Festival of
Architecture
2016

Retrospective

The 'Report Card' of Scotland's Festival of Architecture 2016

Edited by Neil Baxter

First published 2017 by
The Royal Incorporation of Architects in Scotland

Editor
Neil Baxter Hon FRIAS Hon FRIBA

Design
Jon Jardine (mail@jonjardine.com)

Print
FlyerAlarm (www.flyeralarm.com)

ISBN 978-1-873190-76-0

A catalogue record for this book is available from the British Library.

Every effort has been made to obtain copyright release for the words and images within this volume.
For images where no photographic or copyright credit is given,
please assume copyright ownership by the particular partner organisation.
Any enquiries should be to the editor nbaxter@rias.org.uk

Contents

Foreword   5

Introduction   7

Making the Festival   11

Resources   17

Headline Events   19

Partner Events   47

Thank You!   91

Foreword

"The celebration of our nation's architecture is an important part of government's responsibility for the promotion of Scotland's culture. We were delighted to support The Royal Incorporation of Architects in Scotland (RIAS) throughout its centenary year in 2016, along with a very wide range of partner organisations which contributed to making the Festival a huge success. The Festival of Architecture 2016 achieved all of its goals and surpassed many.

The themed Year of Innovation, Architecture and Design was a celebration of Scotland's beautiful built heritage, culture and environment, alongside the contemporary and cutting-edge designs of today. The Festival of Architecture formed a key part of the year, highlighting the many ways in which architecture enriches our lives. Importantly, the Festival engaged and involved young and old and has delivered a legacy of tools and resources for communities, exemplifying the shared aims of the Royal Incorporation of Architects in Scotland and our national policy on architecture and place.

Scotland has been a powerhouse of creativity across the ages, punching well above its weight in the fields of architecture, design and invention. The Festival of Architecture was an exceptional opportunity to interest and involve people and communities all around Scotland and to display what our exceptional built environment offers to the world. This highly ambitious, nation-wide programme of activities enabled people at home and visitors to Scotland to immerse themselves in the wealth of our architectural heritage. Visitors discovered hidden gems and interacted with the Festival in very many creative ways.

Historically our architects have influenced the world and many Scottish architects now work across the globe. Yet, as last year's Festival demonstrated, the quality of our built environment here in Scotland remains a priority for government. Improving the quality of our buildings enhances the lives of all of Scotland's communities."

Fiona Hyslop MSP
Cabinet Secretary for Culture, Tourism and External Affairs

Introduction

"In 2008 the Royal Incorporation of Architects in Scotland (RIAS) determined to mount a public Festival in 2016 marking its centenary. First Minister, Alex Salmond announced Scotland's *Year of Innovation, Architecture and Design* in June 2013. *Shaping Scotland*, the strategy, by the late Stuart MacDonald OBE (1948-2016) and Eleanor McAllister OBE, was published in 2014. The RIAS has only 17 full-time equivalent employees but engaging with members and partners generated a major celebration. The support of the Scottish Government, VisitScotland, Creative Scotland and A&DS, along with all six RIAS Chapters, was key to the success of the Festival.

Chaired by yours truly (Deputy Chair Sholto Humphries PPRIAS), curated by RIAS Secretary, Neil Baxter, directed by Karen Cunningham and designed by RIAS Designer, Jon Jardine, the Festival of Architecture (FoA2016) was co-ordinated and promoted by the RIAS charity.

The Festival of Architecture 2016 was Scotland's largest ever single artform event. Year-long and Scotland-wide, it welcomed over 1.75million visitors, reaching parts no previous Festival has reached. Islands and remote communities held mini-festivals and small towns welcomed visiting exhibitions. 126 partner organisations, including the Children's Parliament, the National Galleries and National Museums, generated over 460 public-facing events.

High quality graphic productions were distributed through Scotrail, the Herald and Times Group and DC Thomson Ltd. The Festival 'brand' was reinforced online. 60+ architectural practices, businesses, Government / A&DS / CreativeScotland / VisitScotland provided funds. "Pump priming" funds catalysed local events. £1.66 million 'cash', and massive goodwill, particularly from the RIAS Chapters and partner organisations, directly benefited Scotland's economy by (at a very modest estimate) over £8.8million.

Although geographically set in Scotland, this was an avowedly international celebration – Bergen, Rotterdam and Vilnius participated in *Cities Expo* (110,000+ visitors). Three versions of *Scotstyle* toured forty venues. The exhibition of Scotland's favourite 100 buildings (1916-2015) culminated in a major public vote (won by Princes Square, Glasgow). There were talks, tours, screenings, performances, educational/children's activities, art shows, crazy golf, music, photography and several touring exhibitions.

All thirty-two Scottish local authorities took part. Numerous educational projects were promoted. Schoolchildren from Tranent met with Kofi Annan, the former Secretary-General of the United Nations, in the European Parliament. Diverse suppliers and logistics partners delivered local events and touring exhibitions:

- *Scotstyle* (forty venues including its final showing at the headquarters of the Royal Institute of British Architects, 66 Portland Place, London),
- *Ideal Hut Show* (twenty 'pimped-up' garden sheds – Edinburgh, Glasgow, Dundee, Inverness Botanics, central Perth),
- *Cities Expo* (five international pavilions, 110,000+ visitors),
- *Adventures in Space* (21,000+ visitors, outdoors 'legacy' version),
- *Out of Their Heads*, Scottish National Portrait Gallery (architect's portraits within twelve gigantic, three-dimensional, drawings),
- *Cake Fest*, Stirling (featured on BBC's *The One Show*).

The Festival of Architecture spawned many mini-festivals. Cove and Kilcreggan enjoyed giant paellas by a local Spanish chef and children's architectural mask-making (enthusiasm undampened by the rain). Parkland and outdoor spaces featured. The revitalisation of Cardross Seminary, presages wide area benefits. Major constructions included the full-scale cardboard recreation of Dundee's Victoria Arch (built one day, demolished the next) static and touring pavilions. A former DC Thomson printworks was brought back to life for a wholly new type of architectural celebration - the joy of the spectacular Festival Finale.

FoA2016 engaged with the broadest public. Funded by the Royal Incorporation (which saved up for eight years), government and sponsorship, the total 'cash' cost was £1.66million. Three books were published. The Festival's legacies include a free website for Scotland's 500,000+ tenement households (*Under One Roof Scotland*) and Scotland's new, annual, month-long, Festival of Architecture (September 2017 onwards).

This unique architecture festival was made by literally hundreds of volunteers – schools, communities and building professionals (particularly architects), their time and expertise, given free – to the long term benefit of Scotland. It demonstrated what can be achieved through the enthusiasm and drive of individuals and organisations pulling together. It also showed how much public enthusiasm there is for the art of architecture, an artform which can truly transform people's lives.

We promised from the outset that 2016 would be fun. It is a year which nobody who was involved will ever forget. And it was joyous!"

David Dunbar PPRIAS
Chair, Festival of Architecture 2016

1950

blished
rovided by
miniscing to a

ws of Robotics,
ulture. A 2004 film
h, is very loosely-
bot, along with
ee!

THE FESTIVAL OF ARCHITECTURE 2016
STRATEGY

Shaping
Scotland

© Malcolm Cochrane

Making the Festival

Towards the end of 2014 *Shaping Scotland,* the strategy for Festival of Architecture 2016, was published. This seventy-two page document, by the late Stuart MacDonald OBE (1948-2016) and Eleanor McAllister OBE set out the vision and aims of the Festival. The document also explained how the Festival would be delivered and described a number of planned highlights of the Festival programme. Remarkably, given the need to raise £1m+ funding and the fairly rudimentary state of preparation of many planned events, Stuart and Eleanor's strategy for the Festival is, in retrospect, remarkably accurate in its predictions. The following extracts and the accompanying graphics detail the vision which with RIAS, the Scottish Government and the group of partner organisations shared for the Festival.

All images © Malcolm Cochrane

Vision

The Festival of Architecture will be a nationwide celebration of how architecture and design shapes Scotland, transforming its places and benefitting its people and their lives. It will reach out to a wide audience, nationally and internationally, inspire and engage young and old, professional and non-professional with a diverse programme of activities, leaving a legacy of tools and resources to help individuals and communities shape their future. **"**

Shaping Scotland 2014, p7

Governance and Management

The organising group for the Festival will be the 2016 Governance Group, involving the senior officers of the participating bodies and funders. A Director will be appointed to plan and manage day to day activities and a further two posts will be created: one to manage the RIAS content, the second to coordinate the delivery of the regional and local programmes. Partner organisations will provide help in kind as part of their activities and there will be part-time posts created to cover the education component, PR, fundraising and IT/graphic design.

The Festival will be represented at the year of Innovation, Architecture and Design Working Group to ensure close alignment with the wider-themed year activity. **"**

Shaping Scotland 2014, p7

Programme Content and Delivery

The programme will be coordinated from the RIAS headquarters in Edinburgh where the Director will ensure that the national and touring activities reflect the overall theme of the Festival. Projects proposed for the national programme including a major exhibition in Edinburgh, *Projects Placed* which will highlight the lives and work of some of Scotland's greatest architects. In the Lighthouse, Scotland's Centre for Architecture and Design, in Glasgow, the proposed exhibition on architecture and science fiction should attract a wide audience. A *Cities Expo* in Edinburgh will feature pavilions reflecting the character and aspirations of invited international partner cities.

Nationwide touring exhibitions will be programmed by the RIAS and its six area Chapters with major public events in each of Scotland's cities and a lively programme in their rural hinterlands **"**

Shaping Scotland 2014, p8

Audiences

Adventures in Space in Glasgow, the *Cities Expo,* Edinburgh and the international grand finale in Falkirk are conservatively estimated to attract 30,000 to 50,000 visitors (source UZ Arts). The RIAS *Scotstyle* and *Ideal Hut Show* are estimated to attract 30,000 and 40,000 respectively as they tour the country (*Ideal Hut Show* attracted 5,000 visitors per week in 1999 in Glasgow Botanics – 20 week tour planned).

The proposed 'build' towards the finale event will involve c. 15 community-based events (estimated audience 2,000 – 3,000 each). Based on the numbers achieved by the *Home* event Falkirk in April 2014, 40,000 visitors over 10 nights of the finale itself is projected (*Home* got 6,000 visitors per night).

Comprehensive PR and marketing will ensure wide circulation of information. Promotional activity will include a dedicated website. **"**

Shaping Scotland 2014, p9

Evaluation

Partners will work together to agree a pragmatic approach to the event evaluation for the Festival of Architecture. A standardised approach to data collection will be agreed and collected by venue/ Hub leads. At key highlight events within the Festival, independent survey collection and economic impact analysis may be commissioned as part of the Festival delivery.

Economic impact analysis for the Festival will use the events industry standard methodology, Event Impacts (www.eventimpacts.com). This methodology focuses on the evaluation of social, economic, environmental and media-related impacts associated with staging major sporting and cultural events. **"**

Shaping Scotland 2014, p9

Aims

The Festival will set out to:

- engage the widest possible audience across Scotland in shaping the thinking and practice of architecture and design,
- contribute to Scotland's attractions as a tourist destination with high quality, unique events with strong international content and appeal,
- celebrate the achievements of Scottish architects and designers nationally and internationally, especially the younger generation,
- raise awareness of architecture's social, economic and cultural importance, past, present and future,
- leave a legacy of tools and resources for individuals and communities,
- underpin and complement public policy. **"**

Shaping Scotland 2014, p14

13

All images © Malcolm Cochrane

Objectives

The Festival will:

- develop an engagement strategy that demystifies architecture and design, reaching across Scotland through a broad partnership network,
- deliver an inspirational public programme that addresses a range of interests and needs, celebrating design excellence, especially the role of younger design practitioners,
- grow tourist visitor numbers across Scotland through a diverse programme,
- create an integrated education, youth and community-led programme with guidance from Education Scotland, PAS and practitioners to ensure best practice to underpin Curriculum for Excellence and meet other strategic needs and outcomes,
- produce a range of tools and resources that will leave a legacy for education and youth and community services as well as design professionals,
- develop new capacities within the architecture and design sectors. 𝅘

Shaping Scotland 2014, p14

Outcomes

The Festival will deliver:

An **engagement strategy** that helps members of the Festival's partnership network to differentiate and target the audience by segments, providing advice appropriate to communities, individuals, visitors and groups, and which provides maximum opportunity for participants to shape their own involvement whether through co-design or social media.

This will be achieved with a series of briefs prepared for each delivery partner and collaborator and a shared IT strategy.

A **public programme of exhibitions, public events, workshops, seminars, lectures, conferences and expos**, Scotland-wide, organised under the thematic umbrella "Shaping Scotland" that facilitates celebration and participation and comprises four sub-themes: Shaping Place; Shaping Potential; Shaping Engagement; and Shaping Global Connections. 𝅘

Shaping Scotland 2014, p14

In addition to detailing how the event would look, the strategy described proposed staffing and how the Festival would be evaluated. It also set out how the event chimed with Government policy and would be measured by this yardstick.

"

To measure performance against Government aspirations for the Festival will involve assessing the quantitative impacts on economic activity, the extent of media coverage, audience reach and numbers of visitors attracted. But there will also be work done to assess the qualitative aspects of the events, such as participation levels, impact on community wellbeing and cohesion and the satisfaction and enjoyment of individual participants. "

Appendices described the proposed governance, and target audiences. Finally, a colourful graphic depicted the planned programme, much of which came to pass (although the Finale, was moved to Dundee!).

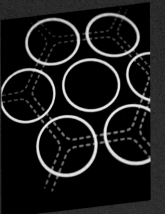

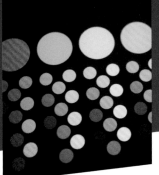

Festival of
Architectur
2016

Meet our

BRAND BIBLE

about th
Festiv

Resources

To ensure consistency in the design of the Festival, the RIAS provided a graphic 'toolkit' online which was shared with all participants. This provided the colour palette for all graphic, print and online productions and guidance on the use of the Festival logo.

Participants were encouraged to submit proposals for events at an early stage, with applications for support finance. Most proposals secured funding from the RIAS with many raising

The third, crucial aspect of the RIAS' support was in marketing and PR. Printed programmes, flyers and posters for the Festival and for individual events were distributed across Scotland and a lively website provided regular event updates. Our PR consultants arranged significant promotional sponsorship from national media and transport companies and ensured excellent press, radio and TV coverage throughout the year.

Headline Events

The RIAS provided an organisational 'umbrella' to coordinate and promote the many and diverse events which made up the year-long Festival of Architecture. However, as its own contribution, the Royal Incorporation also produced two major touring exhibitions, three further substantial static exhibitions, a Scotland-wide architectural bake-off and with its partners at NVA and A&DS respectively, promoted the spectacular launch and closing events.

The following pages review the headline content of the Festival.

Hinterland Kilmahew/St Peter's Seminary, Cardross 18 – 27 March

NVA launched the Festival with Hinterland, an immense public artwork in the ruins of St Peter's Seminary in Cardross. Attracting capacity audiences and international acclaim, the event was a chance for more than 8,000 people to explore one of Scotland's most important modernist buildings, which had been abandoned for 30 years. Hinterland revealed the full glory of the building, combining light installations and projection with a haunting choral soundscape. NVA's long-term plans for St Peter's will rescue, restore and reclaim this outstanding example of 20th century architecture and bring it back into productive use as a national platform for public art. This extract, from a piece in the RIAS Quarterly by NVA's Creative Director, Angus Farquhar, sets the scene beautifully.

"NVA's ambitious scheme to reclaim the future of the world-renowned building and its surrounding landscape represents the last chance to save what is widely recognised as one of the UK's most important post-war modernist statements. Designed and built by Andy MacMillan and Isi Metzstein of the renowned Gillespie, Kidd and Coia, St Peter's seminary was completed and consecrated in 1966. Jack Coia subsequently won the Royal Institute of British Architects (RIBA) Gold Medal for architecture in 1969. However, after 30 years of decline and arson attacks, the buildings are now registered as one of the World Monuments Fund's most endangered cultural landmarks.

What still takes your breath away is the boldness of the original concept, the sharpness of line and the level of experiment through which the two young architects created their homage to Le Corbusier's La Tourette, his 1959 priory for the Dominican Order. Yet there is no pastiche; simple motifs become fluid, free and poetically charged in the new design. Crucial to the continued survival of the main structures, is the quality of the concrete formwork and shuttering which looks as good as it did on the day of construction.

It has taken NVA eight years to reach this first public moment in the resuscitation of St Peter's. That the scheme is led by an independent arts organisation is proof that traditional forms of regeneration sometimes falter when faced with such complex sites.

A dynamic design team comprising Avanti Architects, ERZ Landscape Architects and McGinlay Bell has been appointed to take capital plans for Hinterland forward, adopting a ground-breaking approach to architectural heritage conservation. The scheme combines partial restoration, consolidation of the existing ruin and new design and will create a 600-capacity events space, flexible indoor and outdoor teaching and performance spaces, a permanent exhibition, restored woodland paths, a large historic walled garden and visitor facilities. St Peter's will be a place where ground-breaking new art is produced across multiple platforms and the living heritage is used to inspire debate and the generation of new knowledge."

© Alaisdair Smith, courtesy of NVA

© Alan McAteer, courtesy of NVA

Hinterland was produced by NVA on behalf of Kilmahew / St Peter's Ltd, supported by Event Scotland and Creative Scotland as the official launch event of the Festival of Architecture and a highlight event in the Year of Innovation, Architecture and Design 2016. Supported by Forestry Commission Scotland, Reigart Demolition and Argyll & Bute Council.

Scotstyle

Venues across Scotland March 2016 – February 2017

The exhibition and publication, *Scotstyle* was launched in late 2015 with a call for public nominations for Scotland's best buildings from the period 1916-2015. This public selection process was publicised through digital media, radio, television and communicated to special interest groups.

A panel of ten architectural experts were then asked to select the final list of 100 buildings from all of those nominated by the public. Each panelist was assigned a decade of the century and contributed around 250 words for each of their decade's buildings.

The exhibition had to be capable of being displayed in a wide variety of venues, maximising public accessibility. It required the flexibility to be installed in small venues in remote rural areas as well as large galleries and public spaces in towns and cities. A lasting legacy of *Scotstyle* was the publication of the accompanying book *Scotstyle: 100 Years of Scottish Architecture (2016-2015)*.

Extensive research identified venues that met the objectives of the exhibition. In order to engage with a diverse spectrum of the Scottish public and tourist visitors the exhibition was not restricted to traditional art galleries and museums. Venues included art galleries, a church, civic buildings, community centres, country houses, development trusts, factory sites, heritage centres, an historic ship, historic mills, libraries, major visitor attractions, museums, schools, shopping centres, theatres, tourist information offices, town halls and universities.

The Festival of Architecture's dedicated marketing company helped generate PR through press, radio, television and social media to publicise the exhibition.

The design of the exhibition as three sets of quality 'pop-up' banner stands enabled easy transportation and erection. Shown, through much of the year, at three different locations at any given

1916

1 **Rosyth Garden City**
Queensferry Road, Fife
Greig & Fairbairn and AH Mottram

Construction of the Rosyth Naval Dockyard began in 1909 with over a thousand men employed. Permanent accommodation was required for dockyard workers. The Scottish National Housing Company was formed to build Rosyth Garden Village. Work began in 1915, and the first house was occupied by May 1916. A pleasant garden suburb was created with tree-lined crescents and avenues surrounding a central park. The 'New Town' of Rosyth heralded the way for much of Scotland's public housing in the twentieth century.

1916

2 **Suffolk Road Halls of Residence**
Newington, Edinburgh
Alan K Robertson

The East Suffolk Road Halls were the first student halls of residence in Scotland built exclusively for women. The original intention was to have seven hostels, but only three were completed in the first phase - Buchanan, Playfair and Balfour Halls. The buildings are reminiscent of Robert Lorimer, having an Arts and Crafts air, all satisfyingly grouped around a large lawn. The elevations comprise advanced gabled porches, bow windows and many small-paned windows.

1920

3 **Dutch Village, Craigtoun Park**
St Andrews, Fife
Paul Waterhouse

The fairytale Dutch Village is built on a small island in an ornamental lake. Viewed from a distance it is reminiscent of the chateaux in the Loire Valley where the buildings are reflected in the water. However, there the similarity ends as the buildings in the Dutch Village are white harled with red pantiled roofs, enclosed and linked together by perimeter walls and a columned loggia. Close by is a grotto and a series of three cascades.

1922

4 **Cour House**
Mull of Kintyre, Argyll
Oliver Hill

The greatest achievement at Cour is how the building nestles into its site and appears to rise out of the ground. The entrance front is relatively low and belies the fact that at the rear the landscape steps down towards the sea. The plan is essentially 'L'-shaped with beehive-roofed towers, the whole composition crowned by a series of massive roofs. Stylistically, Cour is a conundrum - it looks both to history and the future. However, it is relaxed and romantic in a wonderful setting.

1923

5 **Zoology Building, University of Glasgow**
University Avenue, Glasgow
Sir John James Burnet with Norman A Dick

The scale of this building belies its size as the various elements are broken up and cannot be readily viewed together. The entrance elevation is small but monumental: it has Baroque details with much use of channelled ashlar; a broken pediment surmounts the doorway. To the left of the entrance is a blank wall forming the rear of the lecture theatre with a tall, decorative louvred cupola ventilator above.

1923

6 **Arches and Extension, City Chambers**
John Street, Glasgow
Watson, Salmond and Gray

The eastern extension to Glasgow's City Chambers was the subject of an open competition. The winning design comprised a block of four storeys with basement and attic whose principal elevation to Cochrane Street is of ten bays. The extension is linked to William Young's City Chambers by a pair of supremely elegant, French Renaissance-inspired, arches. Tall central arches are flanked by smaller pedestrian arches on either side. They create an elegant connection between the original building and its successor.

1924

7 **McLaren Warehouse**
George Square, Glasgow
James Miller

Perthshire-born Miller was one of the most successful Scottish architects of all time. Although strongly influenced by North American architecture he never travelled there. By the end of the First World War, Miller was approaching sixty, but producing a confident urban neo-baroque style. This building is seven storeys with basement, the steel frame clad in pale sandstone. There are only five bays to George Square, half the intended length. Had it been completed, this would have been an inter-war classic.

1924

8 **Bandstand and Amphitheatre**
Kelvingrove Park, Glasgow
Glasgow Corporation Parks Department

This bandstand, opened in 1924, is one of only three in Scotland with an amphitheatre. At the height of its popularity there was seating for 3,000 and standing room for 7,000. It occupies a picturesque location immediately adjacent to the Kelvin, the oval amphitheatre making use of the natural slope of the land. Brick-built with whitewashed render and half-timbering, the building has a red brick base and window dressings, and corniced string course. The stage is framed by tapered Ionic columns.

1924

9 **Winter Gardens Pavilion**
Victoria Street, Rothesay, Isle of Bute
Alexander Stephen and Walter MacFarlane & Co

In late Victorian times an octagonal bandstand stood on Rothesay esplanade gardens. When the development of the Winter Gardens commenced, it was incorporated into the new building as its stage. With a nod to the nearby castle, a circular plan form was adopted. A 25-metre diameter glass dome half envelops the bandstand supported on radial steel ribs culminating in a central boss. Excellent detail abounds. It is an exciting example of seaside architectural flamboyance.

1925

10 **War Memorial and Cowdray Hall**
Schoolhill, Aberdeen
A Marshall Mackenzie and AGR Mackenzie

A particularly fine example of neo-classical work of the period, the war memorial comprises a restrained concave quadrant. Creating the curve is a colonnade of six tall Corinthian columns silhouetted against an inscribed wall under a heavy entablature - all in severe grey granite to underline the solemn purpose of the memorial. Sitting within the quadrant, flanked by steps, is a massive dignified lion sculpture. Inside, and largely unseen by the public, is a beautiful, octagonal, marble-clad hall of remembrance filled with light.

2006

91 **Maggie's Highlands**
Raigmore Hospital, Old Perth Road, Inverness
Page\Park Architects

This centre was developed to deliver an interconnected composition of landscape and built form and sought to 'blur boundaries between internal and external spaces, enclosure and openness.' The centre sits between two spiral mounds within the landscape, creating a trilogy of linked forms, with the building's angled walls clad in striking green copper. The interior space flows and connects into the garden, the sharing of shape and pattern blurring the edges.

2007

92 **Pier Arts Centre**
Victoria Street, Stromness, Orkney
Reiach and Hall Architects

Light spills into this beautiful, crisply delineated building by day and glows from it at night. The heritage of Stromness Waterfront is simultaneously respected and enhanced by a building which both houses the collection within and becomes a crucial part of it. The re-development included refurbishing the existing buildings and adding a striking new 'shed', which has more than doubled the display space of the gallery and enabled the addition of a shop and offices.

2009

93 **John Hope Gateway**
Royal Botanic Gardens, Arboretum Road, Edinburgh
Cullinan Studio

This building takes an organic form, fitting unobtrusively into the Botanic Gardens. It has no obvious 'front' or 'back' since it is intended to be approached from different directions and levels. The extensive use of timber gives the visitor a powerful feeling of 'connection' with nature, enhanced by the glass walls that reduce visual barriers. The timber Glulam roof, the most dramatic element within a series of superbly composed built forms, is set on pencil-thin steel columns - the most slender that the engineering of the building would allow.

2010

94 **Shettleston Housing Association Offices**
Pettigrew Street, Glasgow
Elder and Cannon Architects

The re-working of the early twentieth century red sandstone Co-operative Halls in Shettleston, allied with a new extension providing additional reception, meeting and office spaces (plus an envy-inducing roof terrace for the staff), unites two very different built forms. The concrete-finned extension is a dramatically contemporary response to the older building that successfully integrates with its historic neighbour. The modern elevation, extending beyond its volume to match its historic neighbour, adds to the aura of 'prestige' of this important development.

2011

95 **The Houl**
St John's Town of Dalry, Castle Douglas
Simon Winstanley Architects

The Houl, an elegant, single-storey family home is also 'net zero carbon', utilising a range of traditional and modern sustainable construction techniques to achieve its zero carbon credentials. The building's steel-framed structure is broken up with walls clad in cedar weatherboarding (now silvery-grey) and topped with a seamed zinc roof, cantilevered on all sides to create additional shelter. Within, a functional yet beautiful, red room divider provides a splash of colour.

2012

96 **The Chapel of St Albert the Great**
George Square, Edinburgh
Simpson & Brown Architects

The striking architecture of the new chapel, with its glass walls and 'green' roof, connects it directly with the natural environment of its garden setting. The link between architecture and nature continues in the interior, with timber slats and four, tree-like, Corten steel supporting columns, two internal, two external, which draw the natural setting into the building. The chapel makes a bold and beautiful statement in the rear garden of a townhouse within one of Edinburgh's most historic squares.

2012

97 **House No 7**
Scarinish, Isle of Tiree
Denizen Works

The concept was to rebuild the historic blackhouse in traditional style, adding two extensions modelled on agricultural sheds referencing but certainly not mimicking the local vernacular. The result is a living-house, guesthouse and inter-linking utility wing (particularly useful for cleaning the exposed island's omnipresent sand from shoes). The materials used contrast soft with hard, curved with angular and include stone, corrugated fibre-cement and steel. The stylish interiors feature much use of timber.

2013

98 **The Turf House**
Kendram, Kilmaluag, Isle of Skye
Rural Design

The building is designed to blend seamlessly into the landscape at the northernmost tip of Skye with minimal visual impact. Its turf roof acts almost as camouflage and the larch cladding on the exterior is already beginning to bleach and turn silver with time, again helping the building to blend into its environment. Inside, the home is essentially a single volume with an open plan kitchen/living room and a gallery bedroom platform above. The bathroom, services and main bedroom are ingeniously tucked in below this mezzanine.

2014

99 **Maggie's Lanarkshire**
Monklands District General Hospital, Monkscourt Avenue, Airdrie
Reiach and Hall Architects

Maggie's centres provide a different kind of care. Set in domestic scaled buildings and neither house nor hospital, the plans of the Maggie's centres tend to revolve around the kitchen table. The domestic scale is reinforced by a palette of warm materials, including much national timber. The development is punctuated with a series of courtyards, outdoor seating areas, and a spring that animates the entrance with the sound of running water. In the inner courtyards (open to the sky) are gold-stained 'sun-catchers'.

2015

100 **Laurieston Transformational Area Housing**
Cumberland Street, Glasgow
Elder and Cannon Architects; Page\Park Architects

Public sector housing has changed dramatically over recent decades. This large scale, deservedly award-winning, public housing development learns lessons from the past fifty years. Delivered as the first phase of the masterplan for Laurieston, the project is a collection of 200 properties, including townhouses and flats, all following in Glasgow's long tradition of tenemental homes. The project was praised by the RIAS as an exemplar of successful place-making and "a triumphant piece of urban regeneration."

Images this page © Malcolm Cochrane

time, the exhibition was designed to be light, economic to transport and easily installed with no additional technical requirements. The flexible design, consisting of 12 banner stands, made it possible to configure the display to suit a wide range of exhibition spaces. In total the *Scotstyle* exhibition toured 39 venues throughout Scotland (and one in England) including the Western and Northern Isles.

Scotstyle gained an additional 40 festival 'partners' in the venues which generously waived hire fees and worked in collaboration with RIAS to promote the arrival and display of the exhibition. Travel partner Logan Air transported the exhibition to the Isle of Lewis, to Orkney and to Shetland, allowing the island communities access and engagement with the Festival of Architecture.

For mainland venues the branded Festival of Architecture VW Camper Van (a 1973 'Moonraker') made the transportation of the exhibition as economical as possible when compared with exhibition installation contractors. Consistent branding ensured that a high profile for both the Festival and *Scotstyle* was maintained for the duration of the Festival. Over 10,000 miles were covered in *Scotstyle*'s tour, throughout Scotland.

A lasting legacy has been created with the announcement of the top building of the century as voted by the general public. The winner, Princes Square, now proudly promotes this to the public. The book sold 2,700 copies during the Festival, assisted by sales in the majority of host venues.

The objective of this exhibition was to increase visitor's awareness of architecture and its impact on daily life. Visitor attraction locations ensured that *Scotstyle* reached out to an international audience. By the end of its tour *Scotstyle* had achieved an audience of over 210,000.

© Martin Shields

standard model garden sheds transformed by leading
architects, artists and designers from Scotland and abroad

THE
IDEAL
HUT
SHOW

PRODUCED BY
RIAS | The Royal Incorporation
of Architects in Scotland

SUPPORTED BY
EventScotland

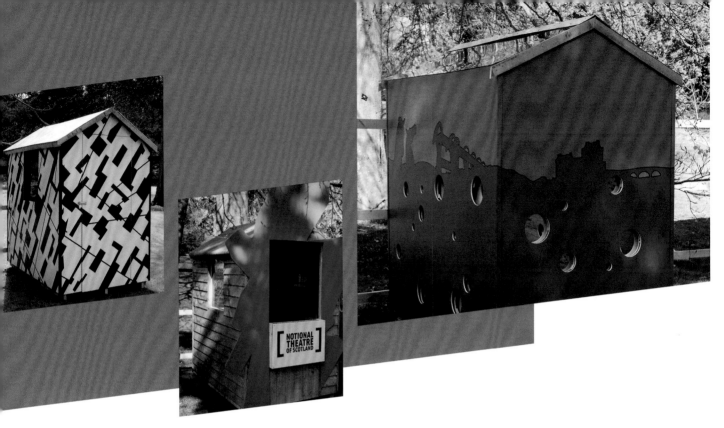

Ideal Hut Show Across Scotland March – August

Originally conceived by Neil Baxter as part of Glasgow's Year of Architecture and Design in 1999, the Festival of Architecture was an ideal opportunity to dust off the idea and curate a new touring version. A list of international architect invitees and leading Scottish artists (most distinguished by their Honorary FRIAS status) contributed their designs for a very modest fee and a competition through the RIAS e-bulletin encouraged healthy Scottish participation.

The exhibition's tour started in the Royal Botanic Gardens Edinburgh, progressing over the following months to the botanic gardens in Glasgow, Dundee and Inverness. The final venue was central Perth, hosted by Perth and Kinross Council. The Council also very kindly ensured that after their last outing all of our 'pimped-up' garden sheds found good homes with local charities and community organisations.

We are very grateful to the architects, artists and designers who created this inspiring show: Craig Amy Architect, Jane Duncan PRIBA Hon FRIAS, Malcolm Fraser, Konishi Gaffney, Isabel and Clara Garriga-Serrano (Holmes Miller), GWS Architects, Jon Jardine (RIAS), David Mackay Hon FRIAS (by kind permission of his widow, Roser), Eva Jiricná CBE Hon FRIAS, Morgan McDonnell Architecture Ltd, NORR, Page\Park Architects, Ian Ritchie CBE Hon FRIAS, John Russell (BDP), Andy Scott Hon FRIAS (Scott Sculptures), Benedetta Tagliabue Hon FRIAS (Miralles Tagliabue EMBT), David Gardner (Holmes Miller) and Adrian Wiszniewski Hon FRIAS.

the architect feel
rather than
? because he
ng a parallel
t i o n

artan hut

engineers like
steelwork
cause it is
t i n g

A room of one's own

Out of Their Heads
Building Portraits of Scottish Architects

All images © courtesy of Scottish National Portrait Gallery

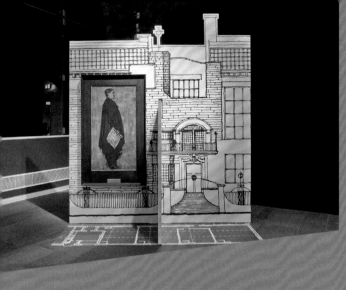

Out of Their Heads
Edinburgh June 2016 – February 2017

Out of Their Heads: Building Portraits of Scottish Architects, organised by the Royal Incorporation of Architects in Scotland (RIAS) and the Scottish National Portrait Gallery (SNPG) and supported by the Scottish Futures Trust, celebrated some of Scotland's most stunning buildings and the achievements of some of the country's most distinguished architects.

This innovatively-presented exhibition, curated by Neil Baxter and Portrait Gallery Deputy Director Imogen Gibbon and designed by Jon Jardine, explored the creativity of a number of key figures who have helped to shape Scotland's world-renowned architectural heritage. Out of Their Heads was built around twelve special constructions, based upon the profiles of buildings by each of the featured architects, drawn by contemporary Edinburgh architect artist Ian Stuart Campbell FRIAS.

Stuart's drawings were exhibited at perhaps the largest scale ever seen in an architectural exhibition. They undoubtedly contributed the proverbial "wow factor" to this show. On each was installed a portrait of an architect – paintings, photographs, drawings and busts, drawn from the collections of the SNPG and RIAS.

Out of Their Heads celebrated the simple thesis that buildings, like any other work of art, originate in the creative imagination of the architect. Twelve renowned architects, from Sir William Bruce in the 17th century right up to Kathryn Findlay FRIAS who only died in 2014, were seen in the context of their creative output. Others showcased were Robert Adam, James Craig, Sir Robert Rowand Anderson PPRIAS, Sir Robert Lorimer PPRIAS, Charles Rennie Mackintosh, Jack Coia PPRIAS, Sir Robert Matthew, Sir Basil Spence, Margaret Brodie and Peter Womersley.

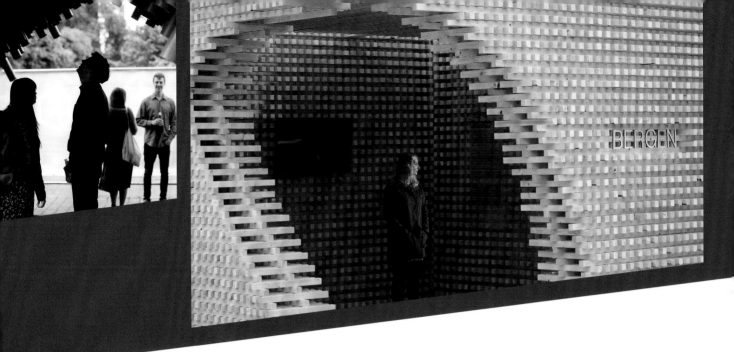

Cities Expo
Edinburgh 21 June – 17 July

Cities from across the globe were invited to design pavilions to be located in Mound Square, the very centre of Edinburgh, in summer 2016. The exhibition, curated by Neil Baxter, built on the universal success of temporary pavilions and the popularity of present-day pop-ups. Architects from Bergen, Dundee, Edinburgh, Rotterdam and Vilnius rose to the challenge of creating innovative and engaging pop-up designs which captured the public's imagination.

With over 25,000 visitors per week at Mound Square, the Cities Expo was by far the most ambitious and successful, public event ever mounted by the Incorporation. The five cities who generously paid for their own participation did us proud. Bergen's pavilion, by a team including the renowned timber designer, Petter Bergerud, arrived on site as ten huge bails of Norwegian spruce two by twos and forty kilos of screws. Visitors commented that what

the Bergen team subsequently produced had a distinctly Japanese quality, its elegant simplicity a testament to the consummate skill of the team which built it.

Dundee and Edinburgh too referenced contemporary Japanese forms. The former was the first building in the UK by V&A architect, Kengo Kuma. Radically different from the Bergen pavilion in its approach, the building, whose executive architect was James F Stephen Architect, had the appearance of a careful stack of logs, fresh from the forest. It provided perhaps the most powerful, olfactory sensation to be found in any exhibition last year.

Inspired by origami, the Japanese influence was again to the fore with Konishi Gaffney Architects' design for Edinburgh, appropriate enough for a practice which originated in Japan and where one half of the partnership is Japanese. Again, predominantly

timber, this layered collection of pyramidal forms was the deserving winner of a competition organised by the Edinburgh Architectural Association for the City of Edinburgh Council. Like the pavilions from Dundee and Rotterdam, this structure was designed to have an afterlife, with various options being considered for its next location.

It seems entirely appropriate that three of the five structures in the Cities Expo were timber buildings. The sponsor of the event, Wood For Good, promotes timber as the default option for all contemporary buildings and the material choice with far the best sustainability credentials.The contrast between the Rotterdam pavilion, an extraordinary construction of angled PVC tubes, and the rest of our Pop-up Expo, could hardly have been more pronounced.

Again a competition winner (its architects, Doepel Strijkers beat off many other teams) its grass roof and planted walls softened the form of what was the most interactive of the five pavilions on show. Open at both ends, its interior formed a shallow pond with stepping stones, much to the delight of the many children who visited and the child in most adult visitors too. The Rotterdam pavilion easily won the competition against Bergen for "selfie central" for the Expo. It also rained indoors when it rained outside (which was for too much of last June!).

Finally, only because this tour is alphabetical, the first city to sign up to take part in our Cities Expo was Vilnius. The Lithuanian capital's pavilion, organised by the Architects Association of Lithuania and curated by Ruta Leitanaite, was a restrained white cube with a cutaway corner entrance. Photographs of buildings and people within, celebrated the vigour and ambition of Lithuania itself and the very special urban qualities of Vilnius.

ADVENTURES IN SPACE

The architecture of science-fiction

Festival of
Architectu...
2016

Adventures in Space

The Lighthouse, Glasgow 7 July – 2 October

When the late and much lamented, Professor Stuart MacDonald OBE produced the strategy for the Festival of Architecture 2016 (along with Eleanor McAllister OBE Hon FRIAS) one of his many inspired ideas was a celebration of the architecture of science fiction films. Stuart thought it could be a blockbuster. It is all the more appropriate that *Adventures in Space* was first shown in the large first floor gallery at Glasgow's Lighthouse, where Stuart was the founding Director. It also featured, in a different format, at the Festival's finale in Dundee.

Science fiction films exert a powerful grip on the human imagination. This innovative exhibition, offered insights into the architecture of science fiction. It considered the startling representations of buildings and cities from movies from the birth of cinema to the present day, including *Blade Runner*, *Flash Gordon* and *The Matrix*.

Brilliantly designed and curated by RIAS graphic designer and self-confessed science fiction geek, Jon Jardine, the show featured over 180 newly commissioned drawings. In addition to a group of

spectacular large scale works (by RIAS stalwart, Ian Stuart Campbell FRIAS) a group of young artists were commissioned to illustrate the key science fiction novels, comics and particularly films, which provided the exhibition's detailed timeline.

Many acknowledge Mary Shelley's *Frankenstein* from 1818, as the start of the science fiction genre. Given that the last of the movies cited was *The Martian* (Dir. Ridley Scott) from 2015, close to 200 years was catalogued in the show. Specific architectural connections are drawn with the works of the Italian Futurists, Le Corbusier, Frank Lloyd Wright and John Lautner.

Perhaps the single most significant influence upon the architecture of sci-fi is the mid/late 20th century American genius, Buckminster Fuller. A collection of his work, recently gifted to the Incorporation, was on public show for the first time, including a number of signed first editions and other early printed works. The form of the show in the exhibition itself paid elegant homage to 'Bucky'.

Metropolis
dir. Fritz Lang

A futuristic urban dystopia, wealthy industrialists reign from highrise towers, whilst poor workers toil below. The city of Metropolis itself is arguably the main star of the film. Its design influenced by New York skyscrapers and Deco Modern, one of the most fashionable architectural styles of the era.

Metropolis became the architectural template for all future cities in cinema, with towering skyscrapers connected by bridges and elevated highways. The streets below are crowded with people, swarming like ants.

Cake Fest

Stirling 11 September

Mid-September brought together keen amateur and professional bakers from across Scotland in the grounds of Cowane's Hospital in Stirling.

Conceived by food innovator and entrepreneur, Simon Preston, Cake Fest recreated some of the most notable works of Scottish architecture in cake across a 100 square metre edible map of Scotland.

A lively packed programme of entertainment throughout the day included a street theatre by the talented Cake Ladies and Tea Club, food tours, live music and, appropriately a number of cake-making workshops.

43

Grand Finale Dundee 18 – 19 November

Although a number of potential venues were considered for the finale, Dundee was felt to offer the best combination of exciting venues and a vigorous city 'buzz'. In mid November, *Light Nights* marked both the official end of the Festival (our programme actually continued until February 2017) and the beginning of Dundee's Christmas celebrations.

Following a theme of past, present and future, the city's historic and contemporary architectural spaces became the focus for large-scale light installations, a torchlight procession, an architectural walking trail, art and design exhibitions and a night market. Over two nights, Dundee's oldest and newest landmarks served as the backdrop for spectacular light shows.

Colourful light installations highlighted the intricate construction detail of Kengo Kuma's V&A Museum of Design, Dundee, creating a beacon of light on the banks of the River Tay. The Steeple, dating back to the 15th century and home to Scotland's tallest surviving medieval church tower was the stage for Biome Collective's interactive sonic light show, inviting people to make music with a building. A 16th century graveyard in the centre of Dundee featured Kathy Hinde's musical flock of Luminous Birds.

Lateral North's 3D timber map of Scotland, presented at the 2016 Venice International Architectural Biennale opened at West Ward Works', a former print factory, alongside other exhibitions including a reprise of *Adventures in Space*.

Visitors to *Light Nights* were invited to join in the atmospheric torchlight procession connecting two of Dundee's best loved buildings McManus Galleries and the Caird Hall. The evening of entertainment also included an installation of giant sized pods, treating passers-by to light waves and massage-like movements when hugged. Created by art duo Colony, the pods directed visitors to Dundee's newest city centre park, Slessor Gardens – also the setting for a festive-themed Night Market, selling food, drink and crafts from Dundee and Angus producers.

Commenting on the event at the time, Will Dawson, Convener for Dundee, One City, Many Discoveries said:

"Dundee is delighted to be hosting the Festival of Architecture 2016 finale. As the Waterfront development progresses it's an ideal time to consider the city in terms of its architectural past, present and future."

Partner Events

Without the work of the RIAS' six area Chapters (Aberdeen, Dundee, Edinburgh, Glasgow, Inverness and Stirling) whose territories cover all of Scotland (including the Western and Northern Isles, Orkney and Shetland) the geographic impact of the Festival would have been much reduced. The reach of the Festival was also hugely enhanced by the vigorous and enthusiastic engagement of numerous partner organisations and other festivals and events which generously sat below the Festival of Architecture 'umbrella' to enhance our special year.

The variety of organisations we worked with collaboratively brought extensive expertise in architecture, design and innovation. Our partners also delivered a wealth of experience in event management, exhibition curation, publishing, community involvement, social enterprise, film, education, project management and conservation. Many of them deliver visitor experiences, exhibitions, publications, online information, heritage interpretation and visitor/tourist attractions throughout Scotland so their contributions helped the Festival attract a huge number of tourist visitors as well as locals.

A full list of partners, including sponsors, is included at the end of this book. We owe them all a huge debt of gratitude.

Aberdeen Society of Architects

Design Matters
Schools across Aberdeen City and Aberdeenshire

18 January onwards

Programme of creative learning events and workshops. The ASA, icecream architecture & The Robert Gordon University, engaged with local schools to develop resource materials for the design element of the curriculum.

© Richard Slater

© Richard Slater

Aberdeen Evolving City Walks + Talks + Workshops
Various locations across Aberdeen

16 – 24 April

Talks and walking tours looked at the history of Aberdeen and the impact of granite on the city's development.

Aberdeen Evolving City Walk
Aberdeen City Centre

16 April

City Centre guided walking tour and workshop by the University of Aberdeen + Aberdeen City Heritage Trust.

Aberdeen Evolving City – Exploring Archives
Aberdeen Town House, Aberdeen

23 April

A step-by-step investigation of the architectural and social history of Aberdeen. An interactive event from Scotland's Urban Past and Aberdeen City and Aberdeenshire Archives.

Aberdeen Evolving City – Become An Urban Detective
Central Library, Aberdeen

23 April

Workshop for 'Urban Detectives' to learn how to investigate Scotland's towns through time.

Aberdeen Fringe Shows
Belmont Filmhouse, Aberdeen

09 – 24 April

A programme of film screenings, Q&As and PechaKucha nights.

© Richard Slater

Fiftyseven Ten
Architecture Lecture
Series
**The Robert Gordon University
Campus, Garthdee, Aberdeen**
1 – 29 April
Series of weekly inspirational
talks by World leading Architects
in partnership with the Scott
Sutherland School of Architecture.

Andrea Deplazes
01.04.16 @ 19.00   57 10

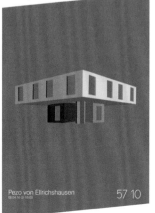

Pezo von Elrichshausen
08.04.16 @ 19.00   57 10

Look Again Mirrored
Pavilion
The Castlegate, Aberdeen
15 – 24 April
A student-designed mirrored
pavillion in the Castlegate acted as
an information point and festival
venue.

Aberdeen Evolving City –
Mapping Your Aberdeen
**Pop-up Mirrored Pavilion,
Castlegate, Aberdeen**
23 April
Participative city model of how
Aberdeen might be shaped in
the future.

A Model City
The Castlegate, Aberdeen
8 – 16 April
Discourse and city model building
reviewing the nature of places
within an urban context.

Agile City

Test Unit: Prototyping Public Space
Centre for Contemporary Arts, Glasgow
7 March – 22 April
A discussion on prototyping ideas and generating change in public space. Speakers included Santiago Cirugeda & Kristian Koreman.

Test Unit: Pecha Kucha 28
The Whisky Bond, Glasgow
7 March – 22 April
A fast-paced evening of talks from influencers and instigators on alternative approaches to city development.

Test Unit: Turncoats - Rip it Up and Start Again
The Glue Factory, Glasgow
7 March – 14 April 2016
An evening of lively debates focusing on the 'mindful mending' of Glasgow's working class and marginal communities.

The Alexander Thomson Society

The Alexander Thomson Society Lecture Series
Glasgow School of Art, Glasgow
23 March – 28 April
Speakers: Professor Dean Hawkes, Fiona Sinclair, Liz Davidson and Mark Baines.

An Lanntair

Building Our Islands
An Lanntair (Stornoway) and various locations throughout the Outer Hebrides
1 – 24 April
An interactive exercise generated discourse regarding the nature of places within an island context.

The ARCHIE Foundation

Oor Wullie Bucket Trail
Across Dundee
27 June
A huge public art event throughout Dundee.

Architectural Heritage Society of Scotland

AHSS Events Programme
Across Scotland

1 January – 29 October

The six regional Groups of the Architectural Heritage Society of Scotland; Dumfries & Galloway, Forth & Borders, Highlands, North East, Strathclyde and Tayside & East Fife each arranged a series of events, incl. walking tours and visits to historic buildings.

© Oban Communities Trust; Rhona Dougall

© Anastasija Sirokova

Architecture & Design Scotland

A&DS produced a lively, year-long programme – engaging with communities throughout Scotland.

Say Hello to Architecture!
Across Scotland

Throughout the year
Events, exhibitions, on-line resources and activities delivered in partnership with community groups and national organisations throughout Scotland.

Best of the Best
Across Scotland

Throughout the year
A touring exhibition featured winning projects from all major Scottish architecture and design awards.

Scotland + Venice
Venice

Summer
A collateral event during the year's Venice Architecture Biennale.

ARCLIB: Architecture School Librarians Group

ARCLIB Annual Conference 2016
University of Strathclyde, Glasgow

6 – 9 July
Librarians involved with architecture and the built environment exchanged experience, ideas and good practice.

© University of Stirling

Association of Scottish Schools of Architecture

Space for Practice
University of Dundee, Dundee
19 February – 24 March
Joint project by the Scottish Schools of Architecture – students as professionals in the public realm, worked in cross-school groups.

Artlink Central/ icecream architecture

Thistles to the Castle
Stirling City Centre
1 March to 25 November
King Street, Spittal Street and St John Street Stirling marking the talent, experiences and places that are in Stirling. Coordinated by Kevin Harrison Director at Artlink Central and Sarah Frood, Director at icecream architecture.

RE:naissance Parade
Stirling City Centre
1 – 30 September
Street Procession combining In Vogue and Community Engagement projects animated Stirling's spine.

Thistle to Castle Commissions: Sign and Street Interventions
Stirling City Centre
1 – 30 September
A series of temporary creative community projcts and artist commissions along the the Stirling route and directing to events for the Stirling Hub Month – included will be projects on buildings, temporary public art, empty shop interventions and performance projects. Included are business sponsored commissions.

Macrobert Arts Centre: A 'Special Building'
Macrobert Arts Centre, Stirling
1 – 30 September
In 1966 the University of Stirling received a donation from the MacRobert Trust of £250,000 for the erection of a 'special building'. This exhibition drew from the University of Stirling's Archive Collection to explore how the original development was conceived.

Aye Write!

Christopher Beanland: *Brutalist Concrete*
Mitchell Library, Glasgow
13 March
A tour of the world's most celebrated and controversial Brutalist buildings.

James Crawford: *Lost Buildings*
Mitchell Library, Glasgow
13 March
The world's lost and ruined structures.

Owen Hopkins: *Breaking the Mould of British Architecture*
Mitchell Library, Glasgow
13 March
Twelve figures from the history of British architecture, including Charles Rennie Mackintosh, James Stirling and Zaha Hadid.

BBC Scotland

Build It!
Across Scotland
Throughout 2016
A programme of activities accompanied a display of Lego models.

Borders Architects Group

Dualchas Architects Talk
Selkirk, Scottish Borders
24 February
Dualchas Architects spoke at an event to celebrate the Year of Innovation, Architecture & Design 2016.

© Andrew Lee

broad daylight

© Tricia Malley Ross Gillespie www.broaddaylightltd.co.uk

Building Sights
Scottish National Portrait Gallery, Edinburgh
11 June – 25 September
Running alongside *Out of Their Heads*, six leading celebrities photographed with their favourite Scottish buildings.

© Brian Cairns

Central Scotland Green Network Trust / Glasgow School of Art

2016 CSGN Forum – The Art of Placemaking
Glasgow School of Art, Glasgow
21 June

The role of artists and designers in placemaking and helping communities, businesses and educational institutions (primary to tertiary) to design green infrastructure and blue and greenspaces.

Children in Scotland

Making Space 2016
Across Scotland
1 April – 16 December

A major architecture and design competition was open to children and young people from across Scotland. An associated international conference also took place.

© Open Aye Ltd / Making Space 2016

© Open Aye Ltd / Making Space 2016

© Children's Parliament

Children's Parliament

StreetsAhead in Tranent: Sharing Stories, Shaping Futures
Tranent, East Lothian
April – November

Children aged eight to eleven considered how their local built environment and the people within it impacted upon their rights and wellbeing.

Cobble Tales

Architectural Walking Tour of Dean Village
Edinburgh
6 – 27 August

Hidden off the beaten track, visitors discovered the legacy of ancient milling industry in a lush valley hidden just beyond the city centre.

Architectural Walking Tour of Old Town
Edinburgh
6 – 27 August

Hidden off the beaten track, visitors discovered the grand and the hidden buildings, courtyards and closes.

Colonsay Festival of Spring

Designing an island: Balfour Paul and Colonsay
Colonsay
9 May
Balfour Paul (1875-1938) designed numerous cottages, a Manse and extensions to the hotel on the tiny Hebridean island of Colonsay. These projects, some of considerable charm and some workaday, show changing attitudes to architectural style and provide an insight into the world of rural estate management in the 1920s and 30s

Denham / Benn

Revolve introduces 'Art Vs Architecture'
Denham/Benn, Ayr
22 – 24 April
Art vs Architecture event as part of the April Open Studios Ayrshire art exhibition. A collaborative exhibition between local artist, Debbie Cassels and Denham / Benn.

© Ross Campbell Photography

Dress for the Weather

Holmwood House Garden Party
Holmwood House, Glasgow
13 August
A family garden party celebrated Holmwood, Alexander Greek Thomson and the Festival of Architecture 2016.

Holmwood Summer Workshops
Holmwood House, Glasgow
26 June – 17 August
A series of architectural workshops around traditional building techniques and crafts.

Celebrating Glasgow's Aesthetic Movement
Holmwood House, Glasgow
1 June – 31 October
A display of furniture and decorative artefacts.

© Ross Campbell Photography

55

Double S Events

ArchiAttack – #SketchTroop
The Lighthouse, Glasgow
5 March
Drawing and celebrating the city's architectural beauty.

#AmeetsA – Architecture Meets Art
Glasgow
8 – 22 September
#AmeetsA is a charity event supporting ABS (Architects Benevolent Society). Created a unique piece of art that celebrates Scotland's architecture.

Dunbartonshire Concert Band

Celebrating the Bandstand
Kelvingrove Bandstand, Glasgow
19 June
The Dunbartonshire Concert Band performed at the Kelvingrove Bandstand and amphitheatre (*Scotstyle* 1924 selection).

Dumfries and Galloway Council

Dumfries and Galloway Design Awards 2016
Througout the Dumfries and Galloway region
1 March – 9 May
The inaugural Dumfries and Galloway Design Awards.

Duncan Tattersall

In Stately Silence: Scotland's other country houses
Mellerstain House, Gordon, Scottish Borders
29 April – 26 September
Exhibition of contemporary art. .

Dundee Contemporary Arts

Grey Gardens
DCA, Dundee
27 February – 1 May
An exhibition of Modernist houses by Morris and Steedman, Peter Womersley's Studio for Bernat Klein and the town art of Glenrothes and Cumbernauld, alongside artists including Guido Guidi, Martin Boyce and Neville Rae.

Diamonds in the Rough: Willie Watt PRIAS
DCA, Dundee
17 March
Experiences as a child of the 70s.

Neville Rae: Town Art in Cumbernauld
DCA, Dundee
20 March
Neville Rae's life-long fascination with the new town of Cumbernauld.

Grey Gardens Salon
Location, Dundee
20 April
An intimate event held in a modernist house built by the Dundee architect James Parr FRIAS.

(((Echo)))
DCA, Dundee
28 April
Series of presentations by local artists and discussion.

Make and break the mould: casting and photography
DCA, Dundee
23 – 30 April
Concrete moulding, casting mini-buildings or sculptures.

Family Art Lab: Balsa Wood and Wobbly Trees
DCA, Dundee
5 March
Led by Architecture students from Duncan of Jordanstone College of Art and Design making architectural models and learning about materials and scale.

Murdo Eason: Fife Psychogeographical Collective
DCA, Dundee
14 April
Read from the recently published *From Hill to Sea, Dispatches from the Fife Psychogeographical Collective*.

Gregory's Girl
DCA, Dundee
20 March
Bill Forsyth's *Gregory's Girl* is one of the most beloved Scottish film ever made. Cumbernauld's concrete architecture immortalised on film.

My Architect
DCA, Dundee
27 March
Directed by Louis Kahn's son, director and narrator Nathaniel Kahn fascinating and touching human story about an architect's life.

Dundee Institute of Architects

Enlightened Dundee
Dundee City Centre
1 – 30 October
A series of evening light projections illuminated the buildings and spaces of central Dundee with architectural stories, poetry and imagery.

Community-Unity Design Gallery
Perth, Arbroath, St Andrews and Dundee
1 – 30 October
A touring gallery of built and unbuilt community projects, celebrated the unity and creativity of communities throughout the DIA Chapter.

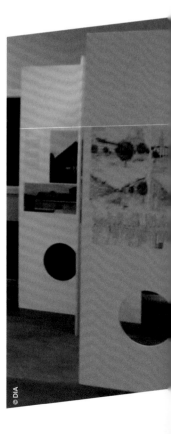

Spaghetti Racecycle
Dundee City Square, Dundee
29 October
Schools assembled a route of drainage pipes across City Square.

Seabraes Yards Design Competition
Dundee
15 – 30 October
Schools and the general public were invited to design a dynamic and striking building within the Seabraes Yards Masterplan, Dundee.

© Malcolm Cochrane

DIA20Y

October

A book celebrated 20 years of Architecture in the DIA Chapter with comments from the general public.

© Malcolm Cochrane

Crazy Golf Architecture

Perth, Arbroath, St Andrews, Pitlochry and Dundee

1 – 30 October

A touring, crazy golf architecture course. You had to hit your ball through nine architects follys to win.

The People's Tower

Slessor Gardens, Dundee

23 – 29 May

Giant (actual size) cardboard representation of Dundee's famous historic Royal Arch. From building preparations to demolition.

© DIA

© DIA

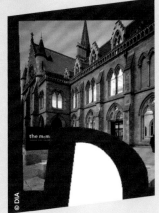

© DIA

31 Days of Buildings

Online and local press, Dundee

1 – 30 October

Images, stories and sketches on-line and tabloid gallery celebrated 31 prominent buildings.

59

Edinburgh Architectural Association

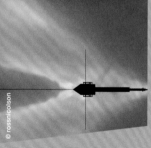

Projection Posters
Old College Quad, University of Edinburgh, Edinburgh
1 – 31 May
Drawings from Historic Environment Scotland printed and posted or projected onto walls.

Unbuilt Edinburgh
Architecture & Design Scotland, Canongate, Edinburgh
3 – 20 May
Exhibition of drawings showing unbuilt major projects in Edinburgh from the last 250 years.

© craigbuchan7

© howden_J

Light and Shadow: Architecture on Screen
Filmhouse, Edinburgh
14 – 22 May
A diverse selection of films about architecture, architects and design. Many coupled with talks and Q&As.

© Courtesy of HES (RIAS Drawings Collection)

Inspiring Spaces Photography Competition
Instagram and Scottish Storytelling Centre (Exhibition), Edinburgh
2 December 2015 – 22 May 2016
Photography competition aimed at celebrating and sharing the favourite built spaces of local people across Edinburgh, the Lothians and Fife.

© rossnicolson

Tradition – The Edinburgh Dilemma?
Royal High School, Edinburgh
29 May

Discussion on the vision of Edinburgh, the dilemma of tradition and modernity, conservation and commercial pressures.

Historical Architectural Films by Murray Grigor
City Chambers Quad, Edinburgh
7 – 8 May

Outdoor Cinema – *The Hand of Adam* and *Space and Light Revisited*.

Architectural Walking, Driving and Cycling Tours
Edinburgh and the Lothians
1 May onwards

Self-guided walking and cycling tours around central Edinburgh, the Lothians, Borders and Fife.

Magical Cities
City Art Centre, Edinburgh
1 – 31 May

Workshops involved school groups and families in re-imagining the distinctive Edinburgh built environment.

Scotstyle
Gayfield Creative Spaces, Edinburgh
14 – 24 May

Exhibition which celebrated the top 100 buildings from 1916-2015, nominated by the Scottish public. This free exhibition toured the length and breadth of Scotland, across all regions, accompanied by a superb new publication edited by Neil Baxter and Fiona Sinclair, featuring the top 100 buildings.

Crafts in Architecture
Gayfield Creative Spaces, Edinburgh
14 – 24 May

Exhibition of craft skills in Lothian, Fife and the Borders, focused on stone, metal, glass, wood, clay and lime.

Edinburgh Central Library

100 Years Young: the Royal Incorporation of Architects in Scotland
Edinburgh Central Library, Edinburgh

23 March

Neil Baxter traced the history of the RIAS from its founding in 1916 as the professional body for all chartered architects in Scotland to the present day.

Edinburgh Chartered Architects Network

ESPC Family Fun Day
ESPC, George Street, Edinburgh

8 October

Family fun day at the ESPC.

Edinburgh International Science Festival

Our Built Environment
Location, Edinburgh

26 March – 10 April

Explored the ways we can build a better world, tackling every scale from the personal to the cosmic through science, innovation and design.

Tiny Homes Village
Mound Precinct, Edinburgh

26 March – 10 April

Tiny Homes Trail transforms a simple roof over our heads into somewhere we are happy to call home.

Playful Cities
Summerhall, Edinburgh

26 March

Investigate why healthy play is important for the adult mind.

A Zero Carbon World
National Museum of Scotland, Edinburgh

27 March

The why and how of zero carbon buildings.

WikiHouse Demonstration Build
Summerhall, Edinburgh

28 March

Build a WikiHouse in an afternoon!

Flatpack in Fountainbridge
Summerhall, Edinburgh
28 March
Architecture for the people, by the people.

Greening the City
Summerhall, Edinburgh
29 March
Urban planning, green innovation and its links with public health.

Utopian Cities: Future Dreams
Summerhall, Edinburgh
30 March
How failed utopian cities have influenced our built environment.

Tiny Home Sweet Home
Summerhall, Edinburgh
2 April
Tiny home developers, psychologists and interior designers discussed what makes a home.

Designing Fictional Worlds
Summerhall, Edinburgh
3 April
How fictional worlds are designed and created.

Future Cities: do they all add up?
Summerhall, Edinburgh
3 April
From architecture to energy to waste disposal – how will the cities of the future operate?

Linking Our Cities
National Museum of Scotland, Edinburgh
5 April
Transport changes that are just around the corner.

Healthy, Happy Cities
Summerhall, Edinburgh
6 April

Bridging the Forth
Summerhall, Edinburgh
7 April
Making the new Queensferry Crossing and looking back at the history of the existing Forth Bridge.

The ARUP Lecture 2016: Meaningful City Infrastructure
National Museum of Scotland, Edinburgh
7 April
Malcolm Smith, Arup's Global Urban Design Leader, explored the importance of 'meaningful infrastructure' in the cities of the

Eyemouth Hippodrome

Making Good Places
**Eyemouth Hippodrome,
Eyemouth, Scottish Borders**
4 August – 3 September
An exhibition where eight
architects explored the qualities of
good places.

Fife Contemporary Art & Craft

Shelters
Kirkcaldy Galleries, Kirkcaldy
5 March – 5 June
Exhibition featuring the iconic
publications of Californian Lloyd
Kahn and Scottish self-builds. It
explored the human need and
drive to make shelter.

Shelters public engagement activity
Across Fife
5 March – 5 June
Tours, drop-in and holiday
workshops for children.

Shelters – Cardboard Den-making Workshop
Kirkcaldy Gallery, Kirkcaldy
9 April
Cardboard den-making workshop
with artist Charlotte Duffy.

Shelters: Lloyd Kahn Talk
Adam Smith Theatre, Kirkcaldy
10 May
Presentation by Lloyd Kahn, Editor
in Chief of Shelter Publications,
California. Championing the
self-build approach since 1970,
Kahn has inspired and empowered
first-time housebuilders around
the world.

© Johnny Barrington

© Johnny Barrington

© Diana Sykes

Findhorn Bay Festival

Findhorn Bay Festival
Various locations in and around the bay of Findhorn, Moray
21 – 26 September
A six-day celebration of Scottish arts and culture, it showcased artists of national and international renown.

Floating Islands
Brodie Castle, Forres
21 –26 September
A pioneering engineered ecology designed by Biomatrix Water of Forres for Brodie Castle Pond.

2020VISION Exhibition
Brodie Castle, Forres
21 September –19 October
Wild Media Foundation's 2020VISION, photographic exhibition documented twenty flagship ecosystem projects.

Guerrilla Lighting Event & Tour
Forres and Findhorn
25 September
Light Collective's Guerrilla Lighting and Light Nights, highlighted the role of light in shaping the night-time character of our built and natural environment.

Friends of Cambusnethan Priory

@Bill Ligherness

200th Birthday of Cambusnethan Priory
Cambusnethan Priory, Wishaw
6 –7 August
200th birthday celebration of Cambusnethan Priory as part of the campaign to save this A-listed gothic-revival masterpiece. Highlighted the lost houses of the Clyde Valley and the architects who built them.

Friends of the Glasgow School of Art

Architecture event for Friends of Glasgow School of Art
Glasgow School of Art, Glasgow
13 October
The Charles Rennie Mackintosh building was severely damaged by fire on 23 May 2014, completely destroying the renowned library. Liz Davidson and David Page discussed how the school has responded to the effect of the fire.

Friends of Wemyss Bay Station

Wemyss Bay Station: Historic photographs and records
Wemyss Bay Station, Wemyss Bay
19 March – 31 December
An exhibition of photographs and records of the construction, history and renovation of Wemyss Bay station and pier, one of the finest railway stations in Scotland.

Glasgow Building Preservation Trust

Glasgow Doors Open Day Festival
Across Glasgow
12 – 18 September
A Glasgow Doors Open Festival Hub for information, talks on architectural innovations and heritage and exhibitions.

Glasgow Institute of Architects

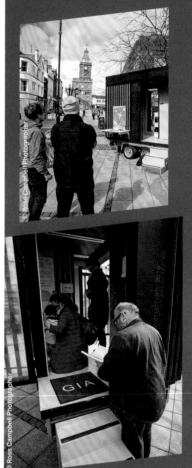

eòlas
Across Scotland
Isle of Coll – w/c 14 March
Kilcreggan – w/c 21 March
Dumfries – w/c 28 March
Glasgow – w/c 28 April
Edinburgh – w/c 25 July
Gaelic word for knowledge. Travelling pavilion promoted architecture and the 2016 festival.

37 Years
Merchant City Festival, Glasgow
30 July – 7 August
A pop-up exhibition celebrated 37 years of Design Awards given to 100 buildings by the Glasgow Institute of Architects.

Talking Buildings
Across Scotland
30 July – 1 September
The public were encouraged to discover 100 Glasgow Institute of Architects' award-winning buildings through a Scotland-wide architecture treasure hunt map.

ScotBuild
Glasgow
23 – 24 November
A retrospective exhibition of all of GIA's Festival projects at one of Scotland's biggest construction expos.

2016 Showcase
West Ward Works, Dundee
18 – 27 November
Exhibition showcased the Eòlas Pavilion and 37 Years exhibition at the Festival finale.

Architect IPA
Launch Event – Drygate, Glasgow
17 March
Holmwood House Garden Party
13 August
The Architect IPA was a limited edition Festival ale celebrating six of Glasgow's most notable architects of the past.

(RE)IMAGINING GLASGOW
Glasgow Short Film Festival, Glasgow Film Theatre, Glasgow
20 March
A short film looked at how Glasgow has been torn down, reimagined and transformed.

Glasgow School of Art

Back to the City: Urbanism, density and housing
Glasgow School of Art, Glasgow
5 – 6 May

The Conference examined the architectural outcomes of the "return to the inner city" – the numerous variations of dense, multi-storey new tenement architecture, and the conditions that generated this architecture.

Greyfriars Garden

Haiku the Noo: Architecture and the Spaces in Between
Shuttle Street, Merchant City, Glasgow
1 May – 18 September

A poetic interpretation of growing food in the city by the gardeners of Greyfriars Community Garden and students from St Stephen's Primary School, Glasgow.

Hidden Door Festival

Hidden Door Festival
King's Stables Road, Edinburgh
27 May – 4 June

The Hidden Door Festival aimed to provides a platform for development of artistic practice, through multi-arts events.

Historic Environment Scotland

366 Days of Architecture
Online
Throughout the year
Daily canmore.org.uk revealed the Building of the Day.

A Tale of Two Cities
Edinburgh Castle, Edinburgh
9 December 2015 – 14 February 2016
An exhibition showed how the cities of Edinburgh in Scotland and Nanjing in China have developed over the centuries. The exhibition was developed by Historic Environment Scotland; Nanjing Museum, one of the largest museums in China; and Nomad Exhibitions, based in Scotland.

Craigmillar Castle Craft Skills Festival
Craigmillar Castle, Edinburgh
27 August
A day of discovery about the ancient craft of stone masonry, included geology tours designing your own stone carving using a bar of soap, a Medieval Construction Science Show and stone masonry with modern day master stone masons!

Edinburgh Castle Rock Containment
Johnston Terrace, Edinburgh
13 January
The stunning Edinburgh Castle towers over the city of Edinburgh resting on a bed of volcanic rock and although it makes for a very dramatic setting, there is a risk of rock fall that needs to be addressed. The District Architect explained the rock containment which is now mitigating the risk of rock falls at Edinburgh Castle.

The Engine Shed
The Engine Shed, Stirling
25 February
A historic building has been updated to become a state-of-the-art learning centre for building conservation.

Urquhart Castle
Urquhart Castle, Loch Ness
17 March
A tour to see the conservation work taking place to the Grant Tower at Urquhart Castle on the banks of Loch Ness.

Holyrood Palace Glasshouse and Gardens
Holyrood Palace, Edinburgh
26 April
A behind the scenes tour of the plant glasshouses allowed visitors to discover how they look after and maintain the Palace's huge array of plants.

Hospitalfield Arts

Autumn Season open weekend project with James Rigler
Hospitalfield House, Arbroath
3 – 4 September
Visitors to the house and grounds saw artist James Rigler's public design intervention.

Inverness Architectural Association (RIAS Highlands & Islands Chapter)

Frozen Music
Highlands and Islands
1 May – 31 August
A photographic event illustrated responses of architecture to landscape and seascape.

Sketch I NESS
Inverness Museum and Art Gallery, Inverness
3 September
An artist-led sketching event in Inverness City Centre. Local artists Catriona Meighan and Clive Brandon uncovered hidden architectural gems and showed how best to capture them on paper.

© Kieran Mead

© John MacPherson

Architectural Guide to the North Coast 500
Publication
1 April onwards
A pocket guide was published identify the architectural highlights of the North Coast 500 route.

Architecture in a Bottle
Caledonian Canal
11 – 15 August
A customised architectural craft was taken along the Caledonian Canal from Fort William to Inverness, playing host to changing artwork along the way.

Mini City/Land of the Giants
Eden Courth Theatre, Inverness
24 October – 17 November
An exhibition of scale models and minature buildings from architects and designers.

Inverness Museum and Art Gallery

Space Craft: architecture meets making
Inverness Museum & Art Gallery, Inverness
5 April – 13 May
A touring exhibition explored the relationship between making and our built environment.

Building Blocks
Inverness Museum & Art Gallery, Inverness
21 May – 18 June
Interactive exhibition designed to encourage school children from across the Highlands to participant in an online building project using the computer game Minecraft.

©Flea Folly Architects

Jakob Jakobbson

At Work
Lillie Art Gallery, Glasgow
24 September – 28 October
A photographic exhibition which showed the epic proportions of major civil engineering projects contrasted against the everyday human effort of construction workers.

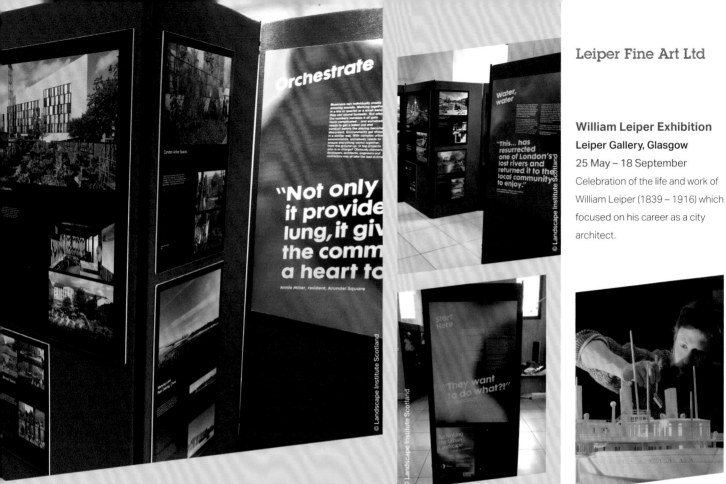

Leiper Fine Art Ltd

William Leiper Exhibition
Leiper Gallery, Glasgow
25 May – 18 September
Celebration of the life and work of
William Leiper (1839 – 1916) which
focused on his career as a city
architect.

Landscape Institute Scotland

The House and Garden of an Art Collector
Royal College of Physicians and Surgeons in Glasgow, Glasgow
29 – 30 September
A design competition for pairs
of designers – one landscape
architect and one architect – to
design a house and garden for an
art collector.

Landscape in the context of buildings
Dundas Street Gallery, Edinburgh
6 – 12 December
An exhibition celebrated the
balance and harmony of buildings
and landscape in Scotland.

Rethinking the Urban Landscape
Edinburgh
1 – 31 July
A touring exhibition which
illustrated the importance of urban
landscape.

LUC

Scotland's infrastructure plan and environmental solutions
LUC, Glasgow office

15 June

A Seminar on "How can Scotland deliver its ambitious infrastructure plan without compromising the environment?"

Maggie's Centres

Culture Crawl
Edinburgh and Glasgow

23 September

Sponsored night walk around Edinburgh and Glasgow allowed participants to the cities' cultural gems, whilst raising funds for Maggie's.

Maggie's to Maggie's
Across Scotland

1 March –31 December

People were encouraged to travel from Maggie's to Maggie's, sponsored to run, walk, cycle or any other means of movement between the centres in Scotland.

Maggie's Just Incase
Across Scotland

1 April – 31 October

An exhibition in a case that told the story, via objects that Maggie's people (architects, key leaders, visitors), would pack 'just incase'.

Melville Housing Association

Dalkeith Corn Exchange Repair Workshops and Seminar
Dalkeith Corn Exchange, Dalkeith

11 –12 October

Workshops demonstated how this Grade A listed building at risk was repaired and converted to Melville Housing Association's main office with community space and a new museum for Dalkeith. Traditional building techniques were demonstrated by Edinburgh College.

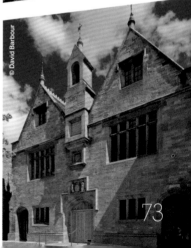

© David Barbour

73

National Galleries of Scotland

Out of their Heads: Building Portraits of Scottish Architects
Scottish National Portrait Gallery, Edinburgh
11 June 2016 – 5 February 2017

This exhibition encouraged visitors to "peer inside the minds of Scotland's greatest ever architects and encounter recreations of their most iconic designs".

Portrait Gallery Architecture Tours
Scottish National Portrait Gallery, Edinburgh
26 June – 25 September

Special tours of the Portrait Gallery were led by architectural historians.

Was Playfair Out of his Head? Building the Architect's Dream on the Mound
Scottish National Gallery, Edinburgh
5 July

Architectural writer Ed Hollis talked about the one place where architects' dreams became reality.

The Architectural Violin with Fenella Humphrey
Scottish National Gallery, Edinburgh
4 August

British violinist Fenella Humphreys presented a wonderfully varied programme of unaccompanied violin music.

Peter Womersley, Authentic Modernism from a Rural Scottish Base
Scottish National Gallery, Edinburgh
10 August

A talk about Peter Womersley, one of the featured architects in the *Out of Their Heads* exhibition.

Inside Out: The Edinburgh New Town Walking Tour
Scottish National Portrait Gallery, Edinburgh
4 September – 2 October

Historian Alastair Learmont lead a walk and talk around the New Town to celebrate the elegance of James Craig's vision for the new town.

Portrait Gallery Curator's Tour: Out Of Their Heads
Scottish National Portrait Gallery, Edinburgh
10 November

Imogen Gibbon, Deputy Director, Scottish National Portrait Gallery spoke about the architect portraits featured in the exhibition.

Build It! – Brick Bingo Challenge
National Museum of Scotland, Edinburgh
13 – 21 February
Some special museum-inspired models and figures were hidden for the public to discover.

Build It! – Big Build
National Museum of Scotland, Edinburgh
15 – 17 February
Master Builders built of one of the museum's iconic objects.

Build It! – Make and Innovate
National Museum of Scotland, Edinburgh
13 March
A series of fun, architecture-based challenges used a range of activities and techniques.

Build It! Adventures with LEGO® Bricks
National Museum of Scotland, Edinburgh
29 January – 17 April
A programme of activities accompanied a display of Lego models.

Build It! Play and Display
National Museum of Scotland, Edinburgh
29 January – 24 March
Children were encouraged to play and create their own model to display for a day. Brick artist Warren Elsmore and his team displayed some of their most beautiful and intricate mini-buildings and models.

Build It! – Live Build
National Museum of Scotland, Edinburgh
3 February – 15 April
Warren Elsmore's team created a large model of the museum.

Build It! – Builders' Yard
National Museum of Scotland, Edinburgh
13 – 21 February
Builders of all ages got creative with LEGO® bricks, big and small.

National Trust for Scotland

The Study House: Bennet House, Culross
Culross, Fife
27 March – 31 October
A learning programme at the Study House demonstrated Conservation in Action.

National Museums Scotland

Architects' Conversations
Presented by the Royal Scottish Academy of Arts & Architecture in partnership with National Museums Scotland
National Museum of Scotland, Edinburgh

The Architects' Conversations series brought together a number of Scotland's leading architects with other leading international architects to discuss shared themes, interests and influences.

Richard Murphy in conversation with Paul Williams
26 April
Richard Murphy RSA and Paul Williams, Stanton Williams discussed 'working with history' in a talk entitled 'All continuity of history is perpetual change'.

Neil Gillespie in conversation with Tony Fretton
10 May
Neil Gillespie RSA and Tony Fretton discussed Abstraction and Familiarity.

Robin Webster in conversation with Sheila O'Donnell & John Tuomey
17 May
Robin Webster RSA, Sheila O'Donnell and John Tuomey talked about 'Context is everything that accumulates around us'.

Hoskins Architects in conversation with Neil Porter
24 May
Join Clare Kemsley, Thomas Bernatzky and Nick van Jonker of Hoskins Architects in a conversation with Neil Porter discussed the theme 'INSIDE OUTSIDE – How do we create a Gesamtkunstwerk'?

John McAslan
21 September
John McAslan RSA and Brazilian architect Pedro Mendes da Rocha discussed architecture's relationship with engineering, art and technique through the work of Pedro's father, Paulo Mendes da Rocha.

David Page
24 October
David Page discussed shared themes, interests and influences in how we shape the places around us.

Spotlight On: The Museum
National Museum of Scotland, Edinburgh
10 November
Celebrated the 150th anniversary of the Victorian museum.

New Lanark Trust

Project Discovery Days – Hard Hat Tours
Double Row, New Lanark
14 April
A unique opportunity was provided for visitors to climb the scaffolding and see up-close the restoration works at Double Row, an eighteenth century tenement block.

Project Discovery Days – Doors Open Days
New Lanark
10 – 11 September
Doors Open Day weekend offered a tour of the World Heritage Site, allowing visitors to learn about the large-scale Townscape Heritage / Conservation Area Regeneration Scheme project.

Traditional Building Skills Workshops
New Lanark
18 May
Workshops offereed visitiors the chance to learn about the traditional skills and materials used to build New Lanark village.

Traditional Building Talks – Scotland's Traditional Building Materials
Mill Hotel, New Lanark
20 October
Moses Jenkins from Historic Environment Scotland celebrated Scotland's Traditional Building Materials, with particular focus on those used at New Lanark.

Traditional Building Talks – The 'Museum Stair'
Mill Hotel, New Lanark
20 October
Allyson McDermott shared her detailed historical research of the 'Museum Stair', a tenement continuously occupied from the 1790s.

Back in Time Experience
New Lanark
17 July
A family-friendly day of games, music, food and entertainment around the theme of life in the 1820s was held in the historic New Lanark.

Building Scotland Exhibition
Visitor Centre, New Lanark
2 June – 12 August
A travelling exhibition provided insight into the diverse materials that have been the building blocks of Scotland's traditional villages and cities.

New Media Scotland

Alt-w: Blush Response
Mobile gallery, travelling across Scotland

14 August – 28 November
New work by Scottish artists toured Scotland aboard the Travelling Gallery visiting five architectural installations that 'blush' in response to their proximity.

Resono
St Mary's Cathedral, Edinburgh

4 June
A music event used the concept of playing the echoes and reverberations of a building or space as if it were an instrument.

NVA

Hinterland
Kilmahew/St Peter's Seminary

18 – 27 March
A world premiere night-time event at St Peter's seminary, Scotland's iconic modernist ruin.

© Alan McAteer, courtesy of NVA

Peacock Visual Arts

'Under New Moons, We Stand Strong' & Urban Knights
Peacock Visual Arts, Aberdeen

5 – 31 May
An installation and performance by the artist Teresa Dillon reflected on notions of resistance and solidarity within the Smart City. Accompanying the installation and performance was a special edition of the programme Urban Knights.

PechaKucha Edinburgh

PechaKucha Night
Nicolson Square, Edinburgh

22 April
A PechaKucha event (20 slides x 20 seconds) which included presentations from Emily Inglis, Annie Griffin, HERE+NOW, Robert Powell and Mike Wilson.

Perth and Kinross Council

© Roben Atoniewicz

© Richard Lea-Hair and Historic Royal Palaces

The Perth Georgian Festival
George Street, Perth

3 September

A series of talks, tours and exhibitions will highlight on Georgian architecture, garden design, fashion, literature and poetry, artists of the period and what life was like in Perth at that period of time.

Inspiring Places: Innovative Design in Perth & Kinross
Perth Museum and Art Gallery, Perth

20 October

Architects, planners and developers contributed to the placemaking process in Perth & Kinross.

Lighting Projections
Perth City Centre

1 – 30 October

Public programme of lighting of buildings and light projections focusing on historic and contemporary architectural images.

A Botanist Looks at the World – The life and work of Patrick Geddes (1854 – 1932)
Perth Museum and Art Gallery, Perth

1 September – 29 October

Exhibition about Scottish biologist, sociologist, geographer, philanthropist and pioneering town planner Patrick Geddes based on a comprehensive collection of visual material from archives, collections and practice research.

The Poppies: Weeping Windows Exhibition
The Black Watch Castle and Museum, Perth

30 June – 25 September

An exhibition by Paul Cummins, Artist and Tom Piper, Designer to mark the centenary of the First World War.

Peta Carlin

Urban Fabric: Greige
Stills Centre for Photography, Edinburgh
22 – 23 April
An installation of photographs of Melbourne's mid-twentieth century curtain wall facades in which the latent image of Harris Tweed was exposed.

© Stills Centre for Photography

Bordering on Genius
The Architecture of Peter Womersley (1923-1993)

This little exhibition gives a flavour of the quality and diversity of the work of the architect Peter Womersley. A London-trained Yorkshireman who spent much of his working life in Scotland, Womersley was among the most distinctive and influential architects of his era. Initially enrolled to study law at Cambridge University, the diverse buildings visited during his wartime experience overseas encouraged him to follow a different career path. During his five year course at the Architectural Association in London, a travelling scholarship funded trips to Austria, Belgium, France, Germany and Italy.

After qualifying Womersley worked briefly with Robert Matthew (later Sir Robert) on the Royal Festival Hall. However, his breakthrough was a house for his brother, Farnley Hey in Huddersfield, inspired by contemporary American modernism, combing rough stone walls with expansive windows. It won a bronze medal from the Royal Institute of British Architects and attracted further commissions, leading to a move to the Scottish Borders.

Among Womersley's first Scottish commissions was the house, in 1957, for the fashion designer, Bernat Klein. Working closely together they created a welcoming, modern, human-scale, family home. Womersley later also designed Klein's studio, one of the most powerfully symbolic modern buildings in 20th-century Scotland.

Womersley's early practice was mainly focused on housing. As his reputation grew, he also practiced for a time in Hong Kong, designing a hotel and apartment complex and refurbishing the prestigious Peninsula Hotel. Over time his work evolved from home-built modernism to chunky and expressive concrete structures, notably at the Nuffield Transplantation Surgery Unit at Edinburgh's Western General and a leisure centre in Coatbridge. Womersley was widely recognised during his lifetime and his projects were published in architectural journals throughout Europe, the USA and even Japan. In recent years this adoptive Scot has become a focus of pride for the Scottish Borders where several of his works survive.

© Colin McLean

Peter Womersley Project

Celebration of Peter Womersley's Architecture in Scotland
Seminar on the 1st of October at the National Gallery, Edinburgh and various venues throughout the Borders
1 – 23 October
The project celebrated Womersley's contribution to Scotland's built heritage. It included an exhibition and a series of workshops which explored Womersley's work, including his collaboration with the renowned textile designer, Bernat Klein.

Pollokshaws Burgh Hall

Guided Tours of Pollokshaws Burgh Hall
Pollokshaws Burgh Hall, Glasgow
17 March – 15 December
A tour of Burgh Hall included access to copies of Anderson's original plans, elevations and sections of the building.

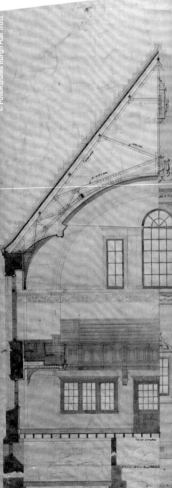

© Pollokshaws Burgh Hall Trust

All RSA Images © Douglas McCaffrey

Royal Scottish Academy of Art and Architecture

HOME: 190th Annual RSA Exhibition
RSA, The Mound, Edinburgh
16 April – 25 May
Exhibition of twenty four interpretations of the notion of "HOME" from distinguished Scottish and international architects. Included innovative completed houses and working ideas for yet-to-be-realised projects.

Royal Scottish National Orchestra

Notes From Scotland
Across Scotland

1 January – 2 July

A national young composers competition from the Royal Scottish National Orchestra invited 12 – 18 year olds to submit a short piece of music inspired by an example of the country's greatest contemporary architecture.

Royal Society for the Protection of Birds

Nature's Architects
Glasgow Botanic Gardens, Glasgow

4 September

RSPB Scotland event showcased the architecture of nature within Glasgow Botanic Gardens.

Baron's Haugh
Baron's Haugh, Motherwell

11 September

Activities involving the wildlife that called the wetland home of RSPB Scotland Baron's Haugh.

Saltire Society

Saltire Housing Awards and Panel Discussion
Edinburgh Centre for Carbon Innovation, Edinburgh

27 June

The Saltire Society's 80th anniversary celebrations included the 2016 Housing Awards, hosted by Kirsty Wark, featured a discussion on the history of the awards.

Building Scotland: Past & Future
Glasgow

7 July

Conversation on architecture in Scotland with Jude Barber, Malcolm Fraser and Neil Gillespie.

Scotland's Jute Museum @ Verdant Works

New Architect Club
Verdant Works, Dundee

15 October

An exploration into architecture for 7 – 12 year olds, used collage and different mark-making techniques to mash up text, logos and repeat patterns into architectural creations, inspired High Mill.

Restoring the High Mill
Verdant Works, Dundee

22 October

A talk and guided tour of the renovated building by a specialist heritage architect who oversaw the project, in partnership with Dundee Heritage Trust.

Scottish Borders Council

© Scottish Borders Council

Scottish Borders Design Award Scheme 2016
Scottish Borders

31 March – 5 September

The Scottish Borders Design Award Scheme 2016.

Reflections: glass : water : art : science
The Haining Estate, Selkirk

30 April – 8 May

Exhibition of contemporary glass art.

Borders Science Festival 2016
Scottish Borders

1 – 31 May

Borders Science Festival 2016 celebrated the wonders of science with educational and creative events.

Scottish Borders Council: Borders Heritage Festival

Borders Heritage Festival
Across the Scottish Borders

1 – 30 September

The eighth annual Borders Heritage Festival celebrated innovation, architecture and design.

Architecture and Landscape Walks at Bowhill
Bowhill House and Country Estate, Scottish Borders

3 – 31 August

Events that celebrated the Year of Innovation Architecture and Design, the Festival of Architecture and Borders Heritage Festival at Bowhill House and Country Estate.

The Great Polish Map of Scotland
Barony Castle Hotel, Eddleston

1 – 30 September

Visitors to Barony Castle Hotel had the opportunity to see the Great Polish Map of Scotland, the largest three dimensional terrain relief model in the world, built by Polish students and local residents of the Peebles area.

Twilight Tours
Across the Scottish Borders

1 – 30 September

Six of the best Big Houses opened their doors for series of Twilight Tours right across the Scottish Borders as part of the Borders Heritage Festival.

The Many Strands of Manor
Tweeddale Museum & Gallery, Peebles

10 – 30 September

Visits to Manor Valley included views of an early Christian gravestone, a Bronze Age hoard, and where Queen Victoria almost bought her Scottish residence.

© Scottish Borders Council

Scottish Catholic Historical Association

Scottish Catholic Architecture and Material Culture
Sacred Heart Parish Hall, Edinburgh

29 October

The conference captured the unique heritage of Scottish Catholic architecture and material culture, reflecting the long history of Catholicism in Scotland.

© Scottish Borders Council

Scottish Civic Trust

Doors Open Days 2016
Across Scotland

1 – 30 September

Doors Open Days gave free access to hundreds of fascinating buildings across Scotland. Every weekend in September members of the public explored places that are normally closed to the public.

Scottish Ecological Design Association (SEDA)

SEDA 100 Sustainable Scottish Buildings Project
Launched October

This publication demonstrated the diversity found in sustainable projects.

SEDA Green Drinks Festival 2016
Edinburgh

1 – 31 May

A festival of Green Drinks events covered diverse subjects such as innovations in housing, the work of Ebenezer MacRae and urban food production.

Urban Expeditions
Inverness, Glasgow, Edinburgh and Dundee

1 March – 30 September

A series of running and cycling routes in each of the five main Scottish cities explored key issues of contemporary sustainable design.

SEDAbuild Bothy
Glasgow and Edinburgh

1 August – 30 September

SEDAbuild, with the help of volunteers, constructed two outdoor classrooms delivered via a series of workshops and courses in both Edinburgh and Glasgow.

SEDA Conference
Comrie

3 – 4 June

The annual conference, in Perthshire, considered 'Small Buildings, Small Footprints'.

Talking Sustainable Communities
Denham/Benn Offices, Ayr

21 April

An evening of informal presentations that discussed sustainability in different communities across Ayrshire and Scotland.

Green Roofs with Dusty Gedge
Edinburgh

17 September

A course on small-scale green roof construction with leading expert Dusty Gedge.

Scottish Mental Health Arts and Film Festival

The Dust of Everyday Life – Architecture and Mental Health
Centre for Contemporary Arts, Glasgow
20 April

The Dust of Everyday Life annual symposium on the arts, mental health, stigma, and social justice, considered how the built environment around us impacts on our health and how architects take this into consideration.

Scottish Opera

The Little White Town of Never Weary
Across Scotland
26 May – 11 June

An interactive musical performance for 5-8 year olds, inspired by the illustrated story by Glasgow Girls artist Jessie M King.

Scottish Society of Architect-Artists

The Vital Art
Forfar, Edinburgh, Glasgow, Stirling, Dunfermline
Throughout the year

Exhibition of artwork by Scottish and European architect-artists celebrated long established traditional bonds between artists and architects in imagining and creating our environment.

Stallan-Brand Architecture + Design Limited

Weather Forms
The Lighthouse, Glasgow
15 April – 26 June
An exhibition that celebrated how Scotland's climate has shaped a responsive and conceptual architecture.

© Helena Fornells

StAnza Scotland's International Poetry Festival

StAnza 2016
In and around St Andrews, Fife (Hub venue at the Byre Theatre)
1 – 6 March
Scotland's International Poetry Festival – City Lines focused on architecture.

Building with Words
1 February – 18 March
Exhibition by Lucy Jones offered unique 'building portraits' of venues and architectural features in St Andrews.

Poetry Assembled
3 – 6 March
A poetic response by three poets to the work of the Turner prize-winning architectural collective, Assemble.

A Window on Poetry
3 March
A festival poetry walk, led by Colin Will, found poems which looked into windows and other openings reflected in buildings around St Andrews.

Within these City Walls
3 – 6 March
Exhibition of four architectural artefacts from the Museum of the University of St Andrews and the commissioned poems responding to them.

© Alistair Kerr

Stills

Lewis Baltz with works by C. Andre and C. Poseneske
Stills, Edinburgh
30 April – 9 July
An exhibition of photographs by Lewis Baltz (1945-2014) alongside artworks by Carl Andre (b.1935) and Charlotte Posenenske (1930-85).

© David Grinly

Steven Blench

Future Heritage – Plastercraft
Fire Station Creative, Dunfermline
3 September
This exhibition celebrated the history and traditions of decorative plasterwork in Scotland.

Stirling Society of Architects

Thinking about the box
Across the Forth Valley
1 – 30 June
A collaboration between architects and communities created thought provoking interventions in our urban landscape in the form of 'cube' installations.

Stone Opera

My Scottish Place
Across Scotland
Throughout the year
Stone Opera was appointed by the Royal Incorporation on a mission to hear about architecture from all. The general public was invited to join their Festival of Architecture 2016 reporters team in this architecture adventure. People were asked to comment on what they thought about their house, their street, their neighbourhood, their town or their city. They were asked to "Film it! Draw it! Record it! Photo it! And then hashtag it" so their favourite places and spaces could be shared with the rest of Scotland. This year-long project engaged with the public of Scotland and demonstrated that this Festival was as much about participation as encouraging new audiences.

Studio DuB

Innovation, Architecture or Design
Studio DuB, West Crosscauseway, Edinburgh
25 April – 29 July
A show of twenty projects: some in-progress, others recently completed and some gems that might never happen.

The Pipe Factory

Daniel Poller: 'Stone Record'
The Pipe Factory, Bain Street, Glasgow
8 October – 6 November
Photography exhibition documented façadism and the adaptive reuse of historical architecture in Scottish Cities.

4 November
Artist Daniel Poller in conversation with Toby Paterson and Johnny Rodger.

The Stove Network

Square Go
100 High Street, Dumfries
29 – 30 March
The Stove alongside a team of local architects, artists and planners created a giant pavement drawing re-imagining the town centre.

Possible Scotland
100 High Street, Dumfries
29 March
Lateral North's touring project, Possible Scotland visited Dumfries in support and to work with the Square Go project.

World Movie Premiere of "A House on the High Street" – Festival of Architecture Dumfries
100 High Street, Dumfries
29 March – 2 April
A premiere of a specially commissioned film by artist filmmaker John Wallace, tracked events leading up to artists collective, The Stove Network opening a public art centre on Dumfries High Street. The film explored the history of the building and surrounding area and asked questions about the role of town centres in 21st century Scotland.

Scottish Scenic Routes Exhibition
100 High Street, Dumfries
28 March – 8 April
The Stove hosted the Scottish Scenic Route exhibition, a project that explored the impact and possibility of small architectural interventions along Scotland's key tourist routes.

UNESCO City of Design

Home
West Ward Works, Dundee
24 – 25 May
Workshops looked at the history of architecture in comics with school children from across Dundee.

© DC Thomson

University of Dundee – Duncan of Jordanstone College of Art & Design

3D's_Design Dens – #3Ddesigndens
Duncan of Jordanstone College of Art and Design, Perth Road, Dundee
17 – 30 October
Pupils' & interior students' from Interiors at DJCAD co-produced architectural structures for local youths to express ideas about their city.

© 3D Design Den

University of Strathclyde

UnCertainty Road Tour 2016
Across Scotland
11 – 16 March
A six day Architectural Road Tour explored art, architecture and cultural artefacts of the built and natural environment.

Strathclyde Architecture International Spring School
University of Strathclyde, Glasgow
5 – 12 August
The S_AISS brought together international students of architecture and practicing architects for an initiative which explored related themes on City and Land.

Urban Memory

Yangon Echoes in Edinburgh
Edinburgh College of Art, Edinburgh
4 July
Writers and specialists in urban history, cultural landscapes and citizenship, were brought together in order to consider the influence that intangible culture has on shaping urban realm.

XpoNorth

Inverness
8 – 9 June 2016
A two-day festival and conference for the creative industries, covered screen, broadcast, gaming, design, fashion, textiles, writing and publishing. Practitioners in architecture took part in the creative mix.

Walking Heads

Glasgow Corner Tour
Theatre Royal, Glasgow
8 June – 31 December 2016
An audio walking tour explored the past and present of some of Glasgow's finest corner buildings and the people who made them.

Glasgow Music Tour
George Square, Glasgow
8 June – 31 December 2016
An audio walking tour explored Glasgow's musical, social and cultural landscape.

Clydeside Promenade
Govan Cross, Glasgow
8 June – 31 December 2016
Using an app for smartphone and tablet the social, cultural and industrial change, was explored in stories told by local people along Glasgow's great river.

Cinema City Treasure Hunt
Glasgow School of Art, Glasgow
16 June – 31 December 2016
A City Treasure Hunt.

Glasgow's Landmarks
City Chambers, Glasgow
16 June – 31 December 2016
A tour of inside stories of great Glasgow landmarks revealed changing fortunes of the dynamic city.

St Nicholas Old Kirkyard: Prestwick Heritage Tour
Prestwick
18 July – 31 December 2016
A tour of gravestones highlighted the dark tales of graverobbers and bodysnatchers, then lift hearts with memories of local heroes laid to rest.

Edinburgh Comedy Tour
Edinburgh
15 August – 31 December 2016
An audio tour of Edinburgh comedy venues that dug into the (sometimes infamous) origins of famous city landmarks.

Barony A Frame audio tour
Ayrshire
12 September – 31 December 2016
An audio tour of this monument in a post-industrial landscape.

A Brisk Walk: Buildings at Risk tour
Sauchiehall Street, Glasgow
20 September – 31 December 2016
The tour revealed hidden derelict buildings.

Thank you!

Producing over 460 events was a huge effort by a very large number of enthusiastic individuals. We thank them all. The list of 'partner' organisations is by way of a thank-you to those who are "too numerous to mention". Some specific acknowledgements, for the headline events, are listed within the texts for each. However, the Incorporation would also like to thank everyone on the following pages most sincerely – and apologise if we have missed anyone out!

RIAS President (during Festival of Architecture)
Willie Watt PPRIAS

Festival Chair
David Dunbar PPRIAS

Festival Deputy Chair
Sholto Humphries PPRIAS

Original Idea / Curator
Neil Baxter Hon FRIAS Hon FRIBA

Festival Director
Karen Cunningham

Festival Designer
Jon Jardine

Marketing and Data Collection
Flourish Marketing
Culture Republic

RIAS Staff
Liz Baillie, Gordon Connelly, Valérie Decker, Gerry Grams FRIAS (for much of the ground work), Carol-Ann Hildersley, Sabrina Leruste, Veronica Low, Emma Lucas, Louise McLeod, John Norman, Sheree Ramage and Laura Sandilands.

RIAS Photographer
Malcolm Cochrane

Festival of Architecture 2016 Governance Group
Karen Anderson FRIAS (A&DS), Marie Christie (EventScotland), Danny Cusick (Scottish Enterprise), Lesley Ferguson (HES), Ian Gilzean FRIAS (Scottish Government), Iain Hamilton (Highlands & Islands Enterprise), Sholto Humphries PPRIAS, Andrew Leitch (Creative Scotland), Ranald MacInnes (HES), Danny McKendry (A&DS), Sandy Robinson RIAS (Scottish Government), Pete Selman (National Trust for Scotland), Helena Ward (Creative Scotland)

Festival of Architecture 2016 Chapters Committee
Dr Gordon Anderson FRIAS, Bruce Ballance RIAS, Donald Canavan FRIAS, Catherine Cope RIAS (nee McKeown), Michael Dougall FRIAS, Isabel Garriga RIAS, Ryan Marshall RIAS, Peter McIlhenny FRIAS, Christine Palmer FRIAS, Ben Rainger RIAS, Ged Young RIAS

Hinterland
Argyll & Bute Council, Angus Farquhar (NVA), Forestry Commission Scotland, Reigart Demolition

Scotstyle
Liz Baillie, Iain Dickson PPRIAS, Helen Kendrick, Euan Leitch, Ranald MacInnes, Ruairidh Moir RIAS, Sarah Pearce, Fiona Sinclair FRIAS, Frank Walker OBE FRIAS, Andrew Wright OBE PPRIAS

Ideal Hut Show
Craig Amy Architect, Jim and Lynn Bryceland (Nairnbrook), Peter Dickson, Jane Duncan PRIBA Hon FRIAS, Malcolm Fraser RIAS, Konishi Gaffney, Isabel and Clara Garriga-Serrano (Holmes Miller), GWS Architects, Jon Jardine (RIAS), David Mackay Hon FRIAS (by kind permission of his widow, Roser), Eva Jiricná CBE Hon FRIAS, Morgan McDonnell Architecture Ltd, NORR, Page\Park Architects, Ian Ritchie CBE Hon FRIAS, John G Russell (haulage), John Russell (BDP), Andy Scott Hon FRIAS (Scott Sculptures), Benedetta Tagliabue Hon FRIAS (Miralles Tagliabue EMBT), David Gardner RIAS (Holmes Miller) and Adrian Wiszniewski Hon FRIAS.

Out of Their Heads
Jim and Lynn Bryceland (Nairnbrook), Ian Stuart Campbell FRIAS, Imogen Gibbon

Cities Expo
Robin Abbey (signwriter), Jim and Lynn Bryceland (Nairnbrook), Alessia Cacopardo, Lindsay Davidson and his team at Forbes Davidson, Peter Dickson, Michael Dougall FRIAS, Clara Garriga RIAS, Alan Gemmell (PHS), Stewart Henderson PRIAS, Kenny Law (Aggreko), John McNeill, Tonde Musunhe, Karen Stevenson
Cities Expo Staff and Volunteers:
Krystle Aunger, Rebecca Bovone, Mark Cousins RIAS, Katrin Dogg Valsdottir, Stephen Freeman, Ken Lochrie RIAS, Eugene Mullan FRIAS, James McLaren, Jilly McLeod, Miguel Fernández Soler, Rob Suttie, Anna Work, Caitlin Wunderlich

Adventures in Space

Jim and Lynn Bryceland (Nairnbrook), Ian Stuart Campbell FRIAS, Ian Elder, Doug Prince, Ciana Pullen, Piotr Sell, Raymond Strachan and the team at the Lighthouse

Cakefest

Simon Preston, his team and all the volunteers and bakers who took part in the heats and on the day.

Finale

Sam Patterson (A&DS), Jennifer Caswell (Dundee City Council), Anna Day (UNESCO City of Design Dundee)

Our Festival Partners

1st Architects; 7N Architects; A449 Ltd; Aberdeen Society of Architects; Acheson & Glover; ADF Architects; Agile City; An Lanntair; An Lanntair Art Centre Stornoway; Anderson Anderson; Anderson Bayne Architects; Anderson Strathern; Arch Henderson Architects; Architectural Heritage Society of Scotland; Architecture & Design Scotland; ARCLIB: Architecture School Librarians Group; Aros Centre, Portree, Skye; Artlink Central; Arts and Business Scotland; ARUP; Association of Preservation Trusts; Association of Scottish Schools of Architecture; Austin-Smith: Lord LLP; Aye Write!; Robin Baker Architects; BBC Scotland; BC Design; BDP; Bennetts Associates Architects; David Blaikie Architects; Steven Blench; Bluefin; BMJ Architects; Borders Architects Group; Borders Heritage Festival; Bowhill Country Estate; British Council; broad daylight; BSP Architects; Built Environment Forum Scotland; Burgh Hall, Dunoon; Shauna Cameron Architect Ltd; Peta Carlin; Caledonian MacBrayne; CBC Ltd; Central Scotland Green Network Trust; Charles Rennie Mackintosh Society; Children in Scotland; Children's Parliament; City Building; City of Edinburgh Council; Clyde & Co; Cobble Tales; Collective Architecture; Colonsay Festival of Spring; Cooper Cromar; Cove Park; Creative Scotland; Crichton Lang, Willis & Galloway; Cruden Group Ltd; Neil Dall Architect Ltd; Dallman Johnstone Architects; Denham / Benn; Design Ark; Double S Events; DoubleTree by Hilton; Dress for the Weather; Dualchas Architects; Dumfries and Galloway Council; Dunbartonshire Concert Band; Duncan Rice Library, Aberdeen; Dundee City Council; Dundee Contemporary Arts; Dundee Heritage Trust; Dundee Institute of Architects; Eden Court Theatre, Inverness; Edinburgh Architectural Association; Edinburgh Central Library; Edinburgh Chartered Architects Network; Edinburgh International Science Festival; Edinburgh Marathon Festival; Education Scotland; Elder and Cannon Architects; Embassy of the Kingdom of the Netherlands in London; Event Scotland; Eyemouth Hippodrome; Falkirk Wheel Scottish Canals; Neil Ferguson Chartered Architect; Festival of Politics; Fife Contemporary Art & Craft; Fife Cultural Trust; Findhorn Bay Festival; Forestry Commission Scotland; Foster + Partners; Denis E Forrest Chartered Architect; Friends of Cambusnethan Priory; Friends of the Glasgow School of Art; Friends of Wemyss Bay Station; Gayfield Creative, Edinburgh; GCA+D Ltd; GGS Architect; Glasgow Botanic Gardens; Glasgow Building Preservation Trust; Glasgow City Council; Glasgow City Marketing Bureau; Glasgow City of Science; Glasgow Institute of Architects; Glasgow Life; Glasgow School of Art; Glentress Visitor Centre Forestry Commission; GLM; GPA Humphries Architects; Grace Food Innovation; Grampian Housing Association; Greyfriars Garden; Groves-Raines Architects; Head of Learning & Programmes NMS; Helensburgh Heritage Trust; Herald and Times Group; Heritage Lottery Fund; Hidden Door Festival; Highlands & Islands

Architectural Conservation Group (previously AIDH North); Highlands and Islands Enterprise; Hill Mill, Dundee; Historic Environment Scotland; HMS Unicorn, Dundee; Honeyman Jack & Robertson; Hoskins Architects; Hospitalfield Arts; Leslie Hutt Architect; icecream architecture; Ingenium Archial; Inverness Architectural Association (RIAS Highlands & Islands Chapter); Inverness Botanic Gardens; Inverness Museum and Art Gallery; Jakob Jakobbson; jmarchitects; John McAslan & Partners; Keppie Design Ltd; Kettle Collective; Landscape Institute Scotland; LDN Architects; Leiper Fine Art Ltd; Leisure & Culture Dundee; Link Housing Association; Lockton; Loganair; Luminate Scotland; Macmon Chartered Architects; MacPhail Centre, Ullapool; MacRoberts Art Centre, Stirling; Mactaggart & Mickel; Maggie's Centres; Mareel Centre, Shetland; Marketing Edinburgh; Marsh (RIASIS); MAST Architects; McInnes Gardner Architects; Melville Housing Association; Morgan McDonnell

Architecture; Moxon; National Galleries of Scotland; National Museums Scotland; National Trust for Scotland; New Lanark Trust; New Lanark Visitor Centre; New Media Scotland; Nicoll Russell Studios; William Nimmo & Partners; Norr Consultants Ltd; NVA; Oberlanders Architects LLP; Page\Park Architects; Peacock Visual Arts; PechaKucha Edinburgh; Perth and Kinross Council; Perth Museum and Art Gallery Exhibitions & Events; Peter Womersley Project; Pier Art Centre, Orkney; Planning Aid for Scotland; Pollokshaws Burgh Hall; Jack Powell Architect; Princes Square, Glasgow; Quigley Architects; Reiach and Hall Architects; Ian Rodger Architects; Ross Smith & Jameson; Rosyth Garden City, Community Council; Rothes Hall, Glenrothes; Rothesay Discovery Centre Visitor Service Advisor; Rothesay Pavillion Project Manager; Royal Botanic Garden Edinburgh; Royal Danish Embassy; Royal Scottish Academy of Art and Architecture; Royal Scottish National Orchestra;

Royal Society for the Protection of Birds; Royal Town Planning Institute Scotland; Russwood; Ryder Architecture; Saint-Gobain; Saltire Society; Scotland's Jute Museum @ Verdant Works; Scotland's Churches Trust; Scotland's Urban Past; Scotrail; Scottish Ahlul Bayt Society; Scottish Awards for Quality in Planning; Scottish Borders Council; Scottish Canals; Scottish Catholic Historical Association; Scottish Civic Trust; Scottish Development International; Scottish Ecological Design Association; Scottish Enterprise; Scottish Futures Trust; Scottish Government, The; Scottish Institute for Enterprise; Scottish Libraries and Information Council; Scottish Mental Health Arts and Film Festival; Scottish Opera; Scottish Parliament Events & Exhibitions; Scottish Society of Architect-Artists; Hazel Smith Chartered Architect; South Kintyre Development Trust; St Conans Kirk, Loch Awe; Stallan-Brand Architecture + Design Limited; StAnza Scotland's International Poetry Festival;

Stewart Associates; Stills; Stirling Council; Stirling Society of Architects; Stone Opera; Studio Dub; Summerlee Museum of Scottish Ind Life; Duncan Tattersall; Taylor Wimpey; The Alexander Thomson Society; The ARCHIE Foundation; The Glasgow School of Art; The Lighthouse; The Pipe Factory; The Scottish Government; The Stove Network; The Voigt Partnership Limited; Tobermore; Tod & Taylor Architects; Town Centre Regeneration Officer; Town Hall Campbelltown; Town House Kirkcaldy; Tranent Regeneration Officer; Under One Roof; UNESCO City of Design; UNESCO Dundee; University of Dundee; University of Dundee - Duncan of Jordanstone College of Art & Design; University of Dundee Botanic Garden; University of Strathclyde; Urban Memory; V&A Dundee; VisitScotland; Vocal; Walking Heads; Wasps Artists Studio; wb_arc; West End Festival; Willis & Galloway; Wood for Good; Woodend Barn; XL Catlin; XpoNorth

Festival of
Architecture
2016

Festival of
Architecture
2016

Braw!

Efter
(After)

Swe/Dan:
Efter

Oot
(Out)

Swe/Dan/Nor:
Ut

Hoose
(House)

Swe/Dan/Nor:
Hus

MANY WORDS IN 'SCOTS' COME FROM SCOTLAND'S NORDIC BACKGROUND.

Braw
(Excellent)

Swe/Dan/Nor:
Bra

Fuhl
(To be drunk)

Swe:
Full

Bairn
(Child)

Swe/Dan/ Nor/Ice
Barn

© A&DS